Foxy and Jost

*...a lively story about a man named Foxy,
an island called Jost, the Tamarind Bar,
the famous Wooden Boat Regatta, and the
Jost Van Dyke Preservation Society...*

by
Peter Farrell

American Paradise Publishing, St. John, USVI

This book is dedicated to the people-- present, past, and future-- of the island of Jost Van Dyke. May their smiles always be warm, their welcome friendly, and their island beautiful.

1st printing July 1993
2nd printing Sept 1993
3rd printing April 1995

(ISBN 0-9631060-4-X)

Special thanks to Keryn Bryan of KATYDIDS for the cover, and to Lani Clark and Vince LoRusso for services rendered.

Table of Contents

Introduction

The Fox of Jost Van Dyke
by
Cap'n Fatty Goodlander

It's no wonder the Virgin Islands are the world's most popular chartering destination. The weather is usually perfect, the sea calm, and the islands-- like green emeralds spewn upon a turquoise sea-- are exquisite. What is amazing, however, is how many people charter in the Virgins year after year after year. When questioned, many of these repeat visitors point to the same little island and the same unique man as the reason for their return. "We came back to sail to Jost Van Dyke again, and see Foxy."

Foxy Callwood is a living legend, a real-life Caribbean myth, a wonderful-waterfront-wacko. He's one of the few native West Indian gentleman whose fame has spread far afield of his small palm-fronded world. You can mention Foxy's name in almost any port on the planet-- in the sleazy sailor's bars of the Azores, the hushed rooms of the New York Yacht Club, or the crowded dinghy dock of a Brazilian whorehouse-- just mention the Fox, and you'll soon be swapping sea stories about the Virgin Islands with a new friend.

Foxy is famous, and deservedly so. The question is: exactly what is Foxy famous for? For owning an island beach bar? For billing himself as the 'laziest man in the world'? For being the world's most laid-back stand-up comedian? For singing for his supper? For having the widest smile?

The answer is not easy. The answer is as varied as his many friends.

"Foxy is a master story-teller," says Lenora Stanciauskas who recently visited the island of Jost aboard a 36 foot ketch from Dutch Sint Maarten. "He tells of large truths in small, simple ways. Each of his tales are multi-faceted jewels, with many levels. He captivates you with his island yarns, until you're hanging on his every word. He's what so many performers wish to be; and so few are. He's spell binding!"

Another visitor doesn't even mention Foxy the Storyteller.

"I love his music," says Lawrence Best as he relaxes in the cockpit of a 52 foot blue ketch which charters out of St. Thomas. "Sure, his songs are funny and they make me laugh-- but they also make me think. Foxy has a unique talent to delight and disturb at the same time. On one level, they're just simple little tunes; on another, they're the stories of universal human folly."

Other guests on the island ignore Foxy's singing and story telling abilities, and concentrate on his business.

"Foxy's Beach Bar has a sand floor, a leaky roof, and not much else," says Captain Mark Rabinowitz of the popular 65 foot charter vessel 'Endless Summer II'. "In spite of that-- or possibly because of it-- it's the site of many of the best parties in the Caribbean. I bring most of my charter guests to Jost, and a visit to Foxy's is the highlight of many of their vacations."

Patrick McGee, off the British racing sloop "Silly McGee", has another viewpoint entirely. "Foxy is not just another 'Turd' World philosopher. He's a Caribbean entertainer in the finest tradition. He doesn't ask for respect, his mere presence demands it. He is blessed with a huge talent, and is driven to share it. He was born to make people smile!"

The island of Jost Van Dyke-- whose population is barely a hundred West Indian souls-- is only a few hours sail from Tortola, St. Thomas, or St. John. Yet it is a "million miles from reality". There was a clock on the island once, but it broke. The biggest local news last year? One of the goats got pregnant...

The island is solely dependent on passing cruising and charter vessels for its income. Nowhere in the Caribbean is the waterborne traveler welcomed more wholeheartedly. Foxy sponsors numerous special events each year to lure vacationers to Jost. His annual Wooden Boat Regatta is one of the most popular events in the Virgins, and his traditional New Year's Eve Party is a world class blow-out not to be missed.

But just why Foxy's Bar is so very special is difficult to define. There's Foxy himself, wrapped in an aura of peace and tranquility so thick you could slice it with a dull rigging knife. There's his lovely teenage daughter Justine who tends bar and shoos away the island children who like to skylark 'tween the bar stools. And there's Foxy's young son Christian who plays amid the bar's patrons in the largest sandbox in the Caribbean.

And of course there is Tessa-- Foxy's beautiful wife of almost 20 years. She was born in England, and raised in Australia. Her fair cheeks blush bright red as Foxy sings a song about his sailing half way 'round the world in an old schooner to woo her. As a couple, they are as different as day and night-- he the outgoing ebony entertainer, she the private wife/mother. "I didn't even know where the British Virgin Islands were until Foxy smiled at me," she shyly admits.

There's a comfortable, "old shoe" feeling about the bar. Locals stop by for a beer. Somebody shows off a fish they just caught: another holds up a giant lobster on its way to a boiling pot. Foxy sings his songs-- often creating epic tunes off the top of his head-- as the seagulls wheel and cackle in the sky above and the fish dart and dash in the sea below. Time seems to stand still. Nothing seems to matter, save Foxy's voice, this moment, the smell of this priceless tropical air.

Each day, boats from around the world gather in Great Harbour. In the late afternoon, everyone rows ashore. To taste a little sanity on a far away island. To live a few golden moments without pretense. To relax.

But exactly who-- and what-- is Foxy? How does he weave his magic?

No one seems quite sure; yet everyone wants to discover his secret. And thus, many lucky sailors return year after year after year..."to sail to Jost Van Dyke again, and see Foxy."

...Cap'n Fatty Goodlander

Where is Foxy's?

It is not down in any map;
true places never are.....
--from 'Moby Dick'

On October 12, 1493-- on his 42nd birthday-- Christopher Columbus discovered the island of Dominica. Shortly thereafter, he came upon the island of St. Croix, which he named Santa Cruz. After duly noting in his ship's log how inviting the island appeared, he anchored his vessel off the mouth of Salt River-- and eagerly went ashore to meet the natives.

Alas, the natives were not quite so eager to meet him. According to Columbus, they were rude. They made threatening gestures towards his group, and quickly chased them back aboard their ship. (This was, perhaps, the beginning of St. Croix's long-standing PR problem with tourists.)

Discouraged at his reception on St. Croix, Columbus once again sailed northward on his ship *Marie Galante*. The following day, he discovered numerous islands-- so many that he named them after the 11,000 Cornish virgins of St. Ursula (who died in Cologne, France, while protecting their chastity from the evil Huns).

For the next few centuries these islands, so piously named by their discoverer, were frequented by some of the most extraordinarily disreputable 'adventurers' imaginable. The beaches were literally awash with rapacious Spaniards, roguish Englishmen, and the dastardly Dutch. Pirates, thieves, and murderers paraded openly down the docks. All the dregs of the so-called 'Western Civlization' seemed to end up in the Virgins. (Many of these original families stayed, with their offspring carrying on their nefarious family traditions-- mostly in the real estate industry.)

The Dutch are credited with establishing the first colony on St. Thomas in 1657. However, they soon departed the area to get in on the ground floor of New Amsterdam-- now known as the Big Apple.

The Danes then moved into St. Thomas, and by 1666 were in full control of the island.

Tortola, meanwhile, was becoming famous throughout the Old World as a buccaneer's paradise. During the 18th century, many of the residents of the big island were engaged in various aspects of piracy. Businessmen, planter, doctors, and other respected members of society openly owned 'privateer' sloops and cobles (also known as *filibusters*) which preyed on passing ships. The whole area was sort of a delightful 'vacation destination' for many of the most wicked members of the 'Brethren of the Coast'.

This continued for an amazingly long period. No one seemed to care. The various European governments nominally in charge were simply having too much fun fighting among themselves to address the problem.

Thus, the bloodthirsty history of this area has filled pages of many a seafaring novel-- and more than a dozen swashbuckling films. The Virgin Islands certainly has a rich, colorful history, and much of it runs red.

Tortola, for instance, has gone through various cycles of wealth and poverty over the years. It has survived its fair share of hurricanes, droughts, famines, rebellions, and war-- not to mention the eternal religious dissensions among its Quaker, Anglican, and Methodist sects.

But nothing remains the same-- especially here in the Caribbean. The island of Tortola, once the most lawless and violent in the area, is now among the most civilized. It is currently experiencing unprecedented growth and prosperity-- due largely to its booming tourism industry.

However, this growth has not been without cost. The once tranquil island of Tortola now resounds with the noise of jackhammers, cement trucks, and jet airplanes. There are construction projects sprouting everywhere-- new buildings, roads, and homes are springing up like weeds. The result is more cars, more trucks, more buses, more taxis, more people, more money-- and, of course, more *confusion* than ever before.

However, just a few miles to the north of Tortola is an island which has escaped such progress. It is still a relatively *unpolished* jewel. Luckily, it possesses neither the glitz of St. Thomas, the trendiness of St. John, nor the cosmopolitan elan of Tortola. For the last five hundred years, it has managed to remain safely outside the mainstream of the modern 'progress' which has swept over its larger neighbors.

It is almost unspoiled.

Not *too* unspoiled, of course. There are a number of good restaurants specializing in local cuisine. There's even a small, tasteful gift shop. Bottled water, ice, and some limited provisions are available at two tiny island-style grocery stores. There are a number of enticing rumshops scattered about its three main anchorages-- there's even a local reggae band and a 'bahn here' Calypso singer.

The name of this wonderful island-- which is 'home' to about 150 of the friendliest people alive in the Caribbean today-- is Jost Van Dyke.

It's an official port-of-entry into the BVIs. The Customs and Immigration office is conveniently located right on the beach at Great Harbour.

Great Harbour is the island's largest and most popular anchorage. It is also the island's biggest 'town'. The main dock is there, and it is big enough to accommodate a couple of dinghies and the local ferry.

While Great Harbour is totally exposed to the south, it is usually quite calm in the anchorage under normal conditions. The Nor'east Tradewinds blow basically from the east, and the ocean swell seldom works its way around the point into the bay.

Great Harbour is widely regarded as the most pleasant spot in the BVIs to 'clear into' through Customs and Immigration. The government officials on Jost are generally faster, friendlier, and more informal than their counterparts on Tortola.

If arriving by boat, don't get too close to the beach. The water shoals rapidly to 3 or 4 feet close in. Also, avoid the channel near the dock. It is in constant use both day and night by the ferries. There is good (anchor) holding here, especially in the southwest part of the bay just inside Dog Hole Point.

While Jost is still a relatively unknown travel destination in the United States and Europe, it *is* an increasingly popular spot for local Virgin Islanders to visit.

The main reason Jost is such a popular spot to 'lime out' and relax on with local Virgin Islanders is primarily because of its *people*. Let's face it-- while no man may be an island, an island is still, well, just another island. What makes one Caribbean island different and unique from another is the collective character of its people-- especially its local characters. Jost is a perfect example of this. While physically no more blessed than a dozen other islands within a dozen ocean miles, its inhabitants seem far more... *relaxed* than their neighbors-- as if Jost was located slightly closer to the Garden of Eden.

The residents of Jost have a well-deserved reputation as the warmest, most welcoming, friendliest people in the Virgins-- a happy island where unannounced visitors are usually made to feel like invited guests.

This didn't just happen. It was planned. The community leaders of tiny Jost realized that if they didn't want to continue to have to travel to Tortola for employment, then they would have to attract their own visitors to their shores.

And in order to do that, they reasoned that they would have to offer their visitors something that Tortola and St. Thomas no longer could-- unhurried friendliness, personal warmth, and pride-of-culture.

They believed that this attitude, combined with the natural beauty of their undeveloped island, would eventually attract enough visitors to their island to provide them with employment.

They had a vision, and they took the long view. Now that vision is paying off.

One of the main reasons for the economic success of tiny Jost is due to the constant efforts of Jost's most famous character, Foxy Callwood.

Foxy is the proprietor (and star attraction) of Foxy's beach bar and restaurant-- but he is also more than that. He is, in the eyes of many Virgin Islanders, a living legend.

His bar, known as Foxy's Tamarind Bar and/or Foxy's Den

of Iniquity, is located on the eastern end of the beach in Great Harbour. It doesn't look like much-- certainly not like it is one of the most celebrated drinking establishments in the entire Caribbean-- which is probably an important element in its long-term success.

For, as everyone who has ever visited knows, 'Foxy' isn't a building of brick and mortar-- but a man of flesh and blood.

Foxy, the man, is also the original founder of the internationally famous Wooden Boat Regatta. This two day event is more than just a boat race for old wooden vessels-- it's a celebration of the vanishing way of life. Both the lovely wooden boats-- and the type of individualistic men and women who sail them-- are rapidly disappearing.

While other Caribbean islands seek to attract upscale, free-spending, hi-tech, globe-trotting, mucho-mega-buck yacht-jockeys to their shores-- the people of Jost come together each year to honor a distinctly different group of sailors.

Foxy's Wooden Boat Regatta is exclusively devoted to all the old funky wooden boats still surviving in the Caribbean today-- and their hard-working, salt-stained crews. Many of these classic sailing craft are former 'warhorses' from the early days of the local chartering industry. Many of the captains sailing in the regatta have been skippering locally for the last 20 or 30 years.

The end result is one of the wildest, most fun regattas imaginable-- and an event which is seldom missed by local sea dogs.

While Foxy's Wooden Boat Regatta began as a relatively local event, it has since grown to major proportions in the last 18 years. It now attracts hundreds of boats, thousands of people, and media coverage from around the world.

Foxy is also the major proponent of the Jost Van Dyke Preservation Society-- which is a home-grown, grass roots conservation movement which aims to preserve as much of the island of Jost as possible in its natural state-- for the ultimate good of both residents and visitors alike.

In many ways, Foxy Callwood is a modern West Indian Renaissance man. While deeply rooted in the soil of Jost, he has also traveled throughout the world. While he cherishes his unique island perspective, he is also intrigued by many of the positive aspects of other cultures. He's a very receptive and open man-- always willing to listen to fresh ideas, always open to all the varied influences which whirl around him.

First and foremost, Foxy is a thinker. He's also a keen observer of island life. These personality traits have led him to question if a lot of things recently undertaken in the name of 'progress' really are. Why should a small island suffer all the ruin and the waste of 'progress' without its people directly benefiting? It doesn't seem fair. So Foxy gradually decided to work towards preventing Jost from suffering such a fate. He did not want to bequeath to his children another Caribbean island which had been paved over, bulldozed down, or sliced up.

Of course, Foxy realizes that the people of Jost have to earn a living-- and for that they need visitors. So, along with his English-born wife Tessa, Foxy and his many friends have worked hard to nurture Jost's unique brand of warm hospitality. And they've succeeded.

To most visitors, Jost is a special place. The island seems to start working its magic the moment you step ashore-- and take off your shoes. (Nobody wears shoes on Jost. It's just not done.) The warm clean white sand seems to pulse with a lilting calypso beat. Everyone is smiling. Everywhere you go, you are welcomed with open arms. The hospitality of the people of Jost doesn't seem like it could be genuine-- but it is.

This is especially true if you happen to come ashore during one of the many carnivals which Jost stages annually. The people of Jost are notorious for how much they love to party.

It is as though Bacchus himself lives just over the hill.

But as lively as Jost can be during one of its many festivals and 'jump-ups', the island is most famous for its peace and quiet. Silence itself is becoming a rare commodity these days, and, thus, an attraction to the international visitor.

Many of the visitors who come to Jost are more attracted by what Jost *doesn't* offer than by what it does.

What is most remarkable about Jost is that it has managed to maintain what the very qualities which almost every other Caribbean island once had-- and yet somehow lost.

Jost has a collective soul. Its people have a sense of community. They are proud of their island, themselves, and their culture. They are confident of their private and public destinies, and thus are able to welcome total strangers into their small world as equals and friends and guests.

The miracle of Jost is that-- because of the warmth and intelligence of its people-- such a Utopian society is able to exist at all.

A Brief History of Jost Van Dyke

As we approach the 21st Century
the people of these islands are ready and eager
to contribute to the progress and well-being
of their country.
They want their children to grow
in an even more prosperous society,
but they are also determined not to pay
the heavy price paid by many of the neighboring islands.
Their caution is one of the many ingredients
that makes these islands and their history so 'different'.

-- Vernon Pickering, author of the
'Early History of the British
Virgins Islands'...

Jost Van Dyke was firmly British in 1735 when the first extensive cultivation of its land began. Sugar cane was the first major crop, but by the 1790's cotton had taken over. By the 1800's most of the sugar plantations, except for a few on the northwestern part of the island, were deserted

William Thornton, who was born on Jost in 1759, returned to the island in 1791. In a letter to his good friend John Coakley Lettsome, Thornton described some of the changes which had occurred in his absence-- in particular the state of Lettsome's birthplace on the island of Little Jost Van Dyke.

Even that far back in time, Thornton speaks of the "sweet melancholy that enwraps the mind when we contemplate a time

16

that *was*."

He called Little Jost 'Lettsome's Island', and described it as being overrun with tamarind and manchineel trees. The island itself was deserted. Lettsome's former home, the mansion built by his father, Edward Lettsome, was in ruins. But Thornton gives a glowing account of the abundance of sea life in the waters surrounding the east end of Jost. Fishing was already the dietary mainstay of those eking out a meager living on the big island.

He also suggested the cultivation of coconut trees for an economic crop, as "they are continually bearing, as one cluster flowers, another is ripening." Coffee could also be grown, suggested Thornton, and other crops might be considered rather than the low profit and labor intensive ones of sugar cane and cotton. (Thornton stated the best coffee he ever tasted had been grown on St. John.)

The BVIs were then primarily Quaker, and on Jost the Quakers had freed their slaves by 1768. (Jost was well known throughout the area as a Quaker retreat.) Even so-- though slavery officially didn't exist after the British Emancipation Act of 1834-- some people within the BVI continued to trade in human cargo with planters on St. Thomas and other islands.

In fact, the notorious Brandenburgers, the German slave traders from Berlin, are believed to have considered taking over Jost prior to their occupying Peter Island.

The Brandenburgers had first established themselves on St. Thomas, but the Danes had quickly tired of them. By all accounts, they were not...er... 'nice' people. And though piracy was openly condoned, if not encouraged, in BVI waters-- at least the booty of the pirates was hard and cold. The idea of selling human flesh was repugnant to most of the people in the BVI, and, as the fortunes of the sugar plantations waxed and waned, not as financially attractive as it might be assumed.

But the BVIs definitely attracted their share of, shall we say, *interesting* characters. Those who went broke or did poorly on islands like Antigua and Barbados often gravitated towards the BVIs. Many were attracted by the freebooting lifestyle and the large number of small islands on which to ply their trade.

Since Jost Van Dyke was named after a Dutch pirate, it seems only natural it became a popular hang out for buccaneers and freebooters. Also, being conveniently out of the way, Jost was a fine place for pirates to leisurely plunder their Spanish treasure ship 'prizes'.

Neighboring Tortola, geographically and topographically a larger replica of Jost, was first settled by pirates anchored in the Soper's Hole area. Some of the more famous sea bandits such as Avery, Roberts, Sprigg, and Edward Teach-- even the famous Blackbeard-- all used the West End of the island as a base at one time or another.

Captains Henry Morgan, George Lowther, and old Billy Bone also headquartered in the area. And Norman Island-- Stevenson's fictional playground of Long John Silver, Johnny Hawkins and Ben Gunn-- was named after yet another pirate.

Though little factual information is known about the particular Dutch pirate Jost was named after, the island has been 'home' to a number of famous people-- in particular William Thornton and John Coakley Lettsome.

William Thornton achieved his fame for being the architect of the Capitol Building in Washington, D.C. Despite the fact that he submitted his drawings to the design contest too late, Thomas Jefferson was so imbued with Thornton's grand concept that it won the honor anyway. Becoming a US citizen in 1784, Thornton became the first US Secretary of Patents.

He also is occasionally credited with assisting with the invention and development of the modern steamboat, and was renowned in his day as a botanist and early geologist.

His theories on the causes of earthquakes and hurricanes are based on studies he conducted with Benjamin Franklin.

Thornton was investigating the possibility that they might be caused by... "electric fluid accumulating in the dry and sandy plains of East Florida or the Yucatan, discharges itself perhaps during the fall of rain, by running on the surface of the sea and passing through the extensive chain of volcanic islands (Great and Lesser Antilles) to the continent of South America."

The above theory has some obvious similarities with modern plate-shifting tectonic theory, and how underground thermoclimes may play a part in earthquake prediction.

But regardless of how good a scientist Thornton was, he surely was a fine observer. "After a severe earthquake it is tremendously awful to listen in the stillness of night to a *second* roaring," he wrote.

Thornton, in his letter to John Lettsome, speaks of the many indicators of earthquakes and hurricanes, saying that the "Ancient Caribes... became such pornosticators of the great changes of weather as to be resorted to by the first European settlers."

His description of one hurricane is classic: "It came on, the clouds began to gather in the Southwest, increasing in density and at last becoming a deep reddish purple. The sea was nearly calm, but as the agitations of the air commenced the sea became violently affected and in a short time rose with rolling breakers mountains high. Its noise and the spray of which was carried over the land half a mile at least by the violence of the wind. Its noise resembled the roaring of a thousand furnace bellows, and nothing scarcely seemed able to withstand its force..."

"It is said the hurricanes usually happen on the days of the change of the moon, the full or quarters, and generally in the month of August. Thus we find agents in the heavenly bodies operating on powers duly arranged in the world for effect."

The Carib Indians-- whose name incidently is derived from the Spanish word 'caribales' which means 'cannibal'-- did far more than merely forecast the weather.

They arrived in the Lesser Antilles from South America, and soon conquered the peaceful Arawaks. (According to recent archeological evidence both tribes may have originally emigrated from central east Asia.)

Regardless of where they came from, like so many other snowbirds do, they eventually ended up in the Virgins. They were interesting people who revered children and enjoyed being polygamous.

Being an independent sort, they considered serving others contrary to their own worth. This probably explains their propensity for suicide when the arriving Europeans attempted to enslave them. They did occasionally practice cannibalism, believing the practice allowed them to acquire their victim's courage.

Today they would probably object to having their pictures taken by cruiseship tourists.

They raided each other, of course, when there weren't enough Arawaks to go around. They soon did such a thorough job on the Arawaks that this group of 'primitives' were hardly in evidence when Columbus and his crew showed up. The Caribs made such a practice of carrying off the Arawak women for wives that in certain villages the women had a different language from the men.

They repeatedly battled the Spanish, Dutch, English and French-- and were notoriously fierce warriors-- but, alas, the Europeans kept arriving in ever greater numbers with ever great fire-power.

The Caribs eventually made a treaty with the Spanish-- and even sold them their Arawak captives for slaves. But the English, French, Dutch, and Danes made no such treaty-- and continued to hunt them down relentlessly. Hopelessly outgunned, the Caribs fought back as best they were able to. By the early 1800's they were effectively finished as a deterrent to colonization.

Today, the Caribs are nearly extinct. Only a tiny settlement of them still exists on a reservation on the island of Dominica.

But back to William Thornton, whose writing is the stuff of Poor Richard's Almanac. (With the influence old Ben Franklin had on him, it's no wonder.)

His physical description of the Virgin Islands-- still timely and interesting after two hundred years-- is from the perspective of the old Thornton estate on top of Sage Mountain on Tortola. It rivals any of the prose you'll find in the modern cruising guides today.

A sample:

"I thence viewed at least a hundred islands and keys rising from the vast ocean.

"Among these to the west at a great distance, may be seen the island of Puerto Rico, one of the finest islands in the West Indies, belonging, but useless to the Spaniards (!); near it Crab Island, or Bieque (Vieques), still nearer to Tortola, the island of St. Thomas, then St. Johns; more to the southwest at a distance, St. Croix. These three belong to the Danes.

"Then we approach by Norman's Island, which with those that follow belongs to the English: St. Peters, Dead Chest, Salt Island, Cooper's Island, Ginger Island, Round Rocks, Broke's Island of Rocks, called the fallen city (Fallen Jerusalem), Virgin Gorda, Dog island and Beef Island, running from the east end of St. Johns a few miles to the south of Tortola, form nearly a landlocked beautiful Island Sound giving a fine stretch of calm water for many miles.

"This sound is called the Virgin's Gangway of the Freebooters, or Sir Francis Drake Bay; he having sailed through it in 1580.

"Virgin Gorda or Spanish Town to the east shows very high land. To the north of the passage between Virgin Gorda and Tortola lie Camanoes, Scrubb Island, the Dog Keys, and

Guana Island; to the west of those and north of Tortola, Lettsome's Island (LIttle Jost) and Green Island, still more west Jost Van Dyke, and far to the Northeast Anegada or drowned island, which in spring tides is nearly under water, and from the southeast point a long stretch of sunken rocks form a most dangerous reef where many vessel are yearly lost."

The man had a way with words.

Thornton, from his vantage point of two hundred years previous, would not be surprised at present day problems. He was against such contemporary practices as stripping the tops of the hills for agriculture, believing the large trees attracted rain.

"So much is rain, at present, " he recounts, "coveted in the Virgin Islands, that after dinner the toast 'more rain' generally washes down 'The King' and 'All Our Friends'."

And he writes his good friend Lettsome that "I have known our countrymen to wish for a *hurricane*, which they say is better than *no cane*."

I, John Lettsome
Blisters, Bleeds and Sweats 'em.
If, after that, they please to die,
I, John Lettsome!

Another famous son of Jost -- actually Little Jost Van Dyke, but we won't quibble here -- was the character in the epitaph above. John Coakley Lettsome, who was a good friend of William Thornton, was born on Little Jost in 1744.

His father, Edward Lettsome, owned the whole island, along with Green and Sandy Key, being one of the original Quaker settlers of Jost Van Dyke in the 1730's. The Lettsomes were part of a group of English planters from Anguilla who arrived in the Virgins specifically to begin sugar cane operations.

John Lettsome left the island early, and went on to become a famous surgeon. He is known as the father of modern medicine, probably due, partially, to his sense of humor.

Old 'John Lettsome -- Bleeds and Sweats 'em' would be destined for some glory. He was in the seventh pair of male twins born to his parents, and the only surviving child of his siblings. Being a Quaker, he, along with others of his faith, freed his slaves in 1768. He remained in London for most of his life, returning to the West Indies only twice.

Thornton, also, didn't hang out much in the islands. Perhaps it had something to do with the consummate disregard the local people had for all efforts to restrict smuggling and the other illicit activities which went along with it.

Of course, piracy has traditionally been an attraction for the poor and downtrodden of the islands. Like the modern T-shirt says, "Smuggling-- not just an adventure, but a way of life!"

There wasn't much else to do, actually. A number of agricultural experiments over the years met with disaster. The sugar business was never as profitable as it was cracked up to be, particularly when it financially depended on slave labor. Cotton turned out not to be viable. (The polyester bush, the nylon potato(e) and the Gore-tex tree were still in the R&D phase.)

There was a brief stab at tobacco production in the Virgins. Cuba was doing it--all those Havana cigars had to be coming from somewhere. But fate swings a heavy machete, and the tobacco beetles wiped the leaves off the plants like Agent Orange.

There was a reprieve-- almost. The United States of America bought St. Thomas, St. John and St. Croix in 1916, then passed the Volstedt Act. This made booze illegal just a scant hop, skip, and a paddle away from the colony of a country which prided itself on its gin, whiskey, and beer.

But don't forget one thing about the people of the BVI-- they are a conservative people.

Sint Maarten jumped in almost immediately, and virtually took over the Caribbean booze trade. The Dutch knew a good thing when they smelled it, and the French knew how to expedite.

Of course, this is not to say that the three Danish islands going gringo wasn't a good thing for the poor islanders across the Sir Francis Drake. A big navy base went a-building in St Thomas, and workers by the boat load were needed. There were some good times.

We know what the major economic boost is today. Over 200,000 *touristas* show up in the BVI annually. This single industry directly employs about a third of the working population. And practically every other economic activity revolves around tourism.

It's boom time in the BVIs. There is even a dredge going all night in Roadtown harbor. During the day there is a constant sound of jackhammers, saws, and drills in the area. Noisy trucks are continuously tearing up and down the narrow roadways, blowing their airhorns at every little turn in the road.

Problems?

The usual. Petty crime. Half-finished projects. Shoddy construction work. The graft and scamming going down that's no different than anywhere else. A sense, occasionally, to this objective observer, that development might be a tad unplanned.

Maybe.

But then that's why people go to Jost.

When there's a cold November in your soul...
-- Ishmael, 'Loomings'
...from 'Moby Dick' by Herman Melville

And now, Dear Reader, it is time to tell you how I, a vagrant sea gypsy by the name of Peter Farrell, came to write this book.

My first awareness of Jost took place on another island-- called Long Island. It was many years ago. The season was late fall, and it was a particularly chilly day...

...I'm standing in the parking lot of a dilapidated bar and restaurant. The place needs a lot of TLC. A faded 'For Sale' sign is nailed to the front door. The building is located in a small, yet undiscovered village on the south shore. We're close to the famous Hamptons here. The hamlet is still a pretty place lying right alongside a body of water known as the Great South Bay. A couple of friends are with me, brothers.

And a real estate agent.

My buddies aren't that crazy about the place. One was in the service with me -- during the recent conflict, as it were.

The year is 1976. The real estate agent's name is Jeff Buck. The little village, still a few years away from boom time, is called Bellport.

We retire to the old Bellport Hotel for drinks, some talk, and to warm our bones. One of the brothers and I will be out early the next morning to fish, whether the bay is frozen over or not. And it probably will be.

Jeff Buck and I have some sailing friends in common, having both grown up on this body of water.

"You're a Farrell, aren't ya?" Jeff Buck asks me.

"Yeah," I said. "But don't tell me you come out of a Jack London story."

He smiled, and began a tale.

The story he told was about a far-away island paradise. It had a quiet harbour, and a pristine beach. There were some dwellings tucked under the palms, and an open air bar with a thatched roof. The bar was a place where, if there was no one about (and often there wasn't) you could go behind the rough wooden counter, make yourself some drinks, and just leave your money in an old jar. He told me of the wonderful character who 'ran' the place, a clever guy he called 'Foxy,' and related some of his adventures.

It was quite a sea story, and one I have never quite forgotten. It stuck with me; changed me somehow. Could there really be a story-book place like that-- in this world-- still?.

A truer tale was never told. And now I'm telling it to you.

Foxy

He had to take an immense
journey in space in order to
achieve a journey in time.
                    -- Sir Kenneth Clark

Jost. We begin at the beginning-- no matter where that may be, as Papa Hemingway once said.

Thus, we begin our tale within the Customs house. The police 'station' is upstairs, while the sandy beach is down below. Though the window to the south, down along the jaws of Great Harbour-- lay the islands of Great Thatch and St. John.

I'm enchanted by the vision outside the Custom's house window. There's a massive black cloud moving between the islands, and though the sound and the fury of the squall is silent, I can see the deluge.

I hope that St. John (me home, mon!) is getting its fair share of rain.

But I am here to request official 'clearance' into Jost, despite my natural fear and trepidation of dealing with authority figures. This started somewhere in kindergarten, I know, when I was constantly reproached for liberating those blackboard erasers, and for swiping those stupid wood blocks for use as blockade-runners and gun-smuggling vessels. I even admit to appropriating the occasional sandbox also. Hell, I wanted my private ocean just like Sir Francis Drake...

"Occupation?"

"Er, writer," I tell the Custom's man. Some wag in the background is whistling Arlo Guthrie... *don't touch my bags, if you please, Mr. Customs Man*! Or is that just my natural paranoid singing?

He smiled so broadly for a moment he almost forgot himself. "Petah," he said. "You a *writer*, now, you are sayin'?"

"Well, I've been known to do it, you know."

They kind of know me here. I've been coming to Jost for a number of years now, usually as crew or captain on someone else's boat. I've attended a few Wooden Boat Regattas, done the carnivals, made a complete ass of myself at Laury's, Foxy's, Rudy's-- once I was even surprised by a member of the Royal Family (won't tell which one!) while taking a leak on Sandy Cay...

And so it began.

We went through the usual passport-and-boat-registration ritual, which I won't get into. It doesn't take long. The people here are friendly, but make sure you properly clear in-- or they won't be when they find out.

Then it was eastward down the beach to Foxy's.

"They call shark here 'flake,'" Tessa said, her Aussie accent tinged slightly with the clipped King's English of her birthplace. "You can order shark in all the restaurants around Melbourne. But here," and she sighed, "they don't like the smell of it, you know. Plus they're big! We've caught some right around the point over here--"

She gestured out past the bar to the mouth of Great Harbour. I was seated on a wooden stool at Foxy's bar, just Tessa and I. We were talking about her children, her life, and her husband-- Foxy Callwood.

Tessa Callwood is blond, thin and graceful. She has that peculiarly English wistful beauty that transcends years. Her easy demeanor makes one feel instantly accepted.

Her younger children, Jemilla and Christian, 8 and 9, were ranging in and out of the kitchen back behind the bar. They were playing with some kittens, their high sing-song voices blending in with the sounds of the afternoon. She and Foxy also have an older daughter, Justine, 19 years old, who is currently attending Lehigh University in Pennsylvania.

Tessa told me about living in a suburb of Melbourne, where her parents had emigrated when she was still a child. She had gone to Melbourne University, and then began to travel..

But then she bumped into Foxy in Gibraltar...

And then Foxy himself ambled into the bar. We shook hands and assayed each other-- me the 'Honky Gonzo Journalist,' and Foxy as the 'Subject.'

He'd seen me around before-- just another charter captain, booze-hound, and skirt-chaser-- similar to thousands of others who have passed through his bar in the past twenty years he's been in business.

Philicianno "Foxy" Callwood is tall and very dark, with classic West Indian features-- no longer really African, but no Caucasian blood there either that's discernible. His hair is in semi-dreads, his mouth in a constant whimsical smile, and his eyes look directly at you with a constant humor, as though, whatever happens, this will be fun. He has long, spatulate fingers, his hands rough feeling and strong-- working hands.

He was still smiling now, but those eyes were suddenly serious. With a proud astuteness, he slid a slim piece of paper across the bar towards me. It looked like a brochure of some type. I glanced at it quickly, noticing the logo on top--a sketch of Jost with a giant coconut palm growing out of it, with the words JOST VAN DYKE PRESERVATION SOCIETY.

A description of just what the J.V.D.P.S. is all about followed. On the bottom, in bold type, it stated: SO! -- DO YOU CARE? IT'S FUTURE DEPENDS ON YOU! The other side was reserved for your name and address, etc. and a request for whatever support one could offer. On the bottom here, in boldface again, was the statement, A WARM PLACE NOT ONLY IN OUR WORLD... BUT IN YOUR HEART, LET'S PASS IT ON.

But then Foxy laughed, pushed another Heineken my way, grabbed his guitar, and proceeded to 'work.' Like the man said when I asked him how many songs he's written down (none), "It's work. I came to work now."

And the man began to play as some touristas began drifting in. They were led by an elderly couple who had their children with them, and their children's children, making up quite a camp. They comfortably ensconced themselves as though in their own living rooms-- safe in St. Paul or Scarsdale-- not in this strange, third world beach hut where the only other patrons were probably bandits, pirates, writers or worse...

But the intimacy in the place was, well, convincing. There's a special aura which clings to Foxy-- a certain personal warmth. It's easy to feel safe and welcome in his presence.

Of course, whenever I approached Tessa directly about the 'Subject," she casually shuffles my questions aside.

Now Foxy is singing...

"...without a flash,
your camera would crash.
For it won't have been me,
for there will be,
only a blank spot where I was supposed to be!
Oh, dee dee dah, O dee dee doh..."

Foxy's voice has a certain cadence, a unique West Indian rhythm which flows through it. It is a clean strong voice; a good instrument for singing, story-telling, or making a conversational point. Foxy wants you to hear him.

It is interesting to watch visitors step ashore on Jost for the first time. Many look like the native goats foraging for food as they step off the dock to explore the island. They usually begin by ranging aimless up and down the beach, as if they're expecting to discover a modern town lurking behind the next palm tree.

But, of course, there is no town on Jost. The beach of Great Harbour, less than a 1/4 mile long, is all there is. And its enough. It's a picture-postcard beach, so clean and white and dazzling that it almost hurts the eye.

There's a number of island bars along its short stretch. Surely no one has ever died of thirst on Jost. Each bar carries all the usual native crafts, T-shirts, and other plastic junk to which tourists everywhere are attracted to.

Almost immediately the visitor realizes that almost no one on Jost is wearing shoes. This makes perfect sense when the main street is a beach. Somehow, being barefoot is relaxing.

There's nothing high-tech here. In the heat of the afternoon a few dogs loll about. There might be some bikinied women splashing about in the crystal-clear water just off the beach. And as you meander along, past the beach front saloons and resting places, a dark figure or two relaxing in the shade within might say, "Hey!" in greeting, or "All right..!"

And that's about it.

There's a few boats up on the beach, under the trees, usually being repaired. A man or two may be puttering about, dabbing on a spot of fiberglass resin here and there, or maybe even replacing a plank. He is working on island time, and is in no big rush. Everyone says 'Hello" in their own inimitable fashion, however, and will even step aside for you to inspect their work. For the most part, the people of Jost are a friendly people, happy in what they are doing.

They will also be happy to give you advice on just about any subject-- like where's a good place to snorkel (around the point just off the reef), a good place to fish (anywhere), a place to get a sandwich (a nod of the head up and down the beach to anyone of a half-dozen places).

And down near the end of the beach there is someone playing

a guitar and singing:

> Yea, yea, yea--you look very good,
> Like you from a place called Hollywood!
> I only wish she would not be hurt.
> I suspected dat just from her shirt!
> An' because you look like Ulysses Grant,
> I only know this from your hair transplant!
> But I tell ya man, it ain't no disgrace
> 'Cause Mother Nature take your hair and plant it on your
> > face
> And I only hope, you not feelin' blue
> 'Cause Mother Nature perform the same operation on me
> > too!
> Dah dah dah, dah dah dee...

Yes, it's Foxy. He's playing for some people sitting around the bar. Most of the kids present are sipping sodas, while their parents usually have a rum drink in their hand. And the totally impromptu song Foxy just sang off the top of his head was for a couple who just finished a lunch of roti and fish soup.

For Foxy is that type of singular good will ambassador that won't let someone leave his place without a smile on their face and a warm feeling in their heart. He'll sing about anything that comes to mind, whether politics, the heat, or where someone happens to call home. He's travelled enough and seen enough to be as well versed as someone who reads the New York Times every morning before their 'power breakfast'. And he begins his tales in such a way to throw off even the most baleful glare.

"Ya know, I got an adventure I'd like to share with you all. That's the adventure of finding a wife. This happened over twenty years ago. I had these four sons-- they were born two one year, two the next year."

Some titters from the benches--

"No, no!" Foxy remands, grinning ear to ear, his fingers picking out a tune on the guitar. "No twins or nothing like that! You see, at that time here there was no television or nothing like that here on the island.

"Anyway, after that, I couldn't find a girlfriend around here to save my life! So, whenever a boat would sail in, and the captain would have a gorgeous cook on board, I would always try to get them to spend the weekend ashore with me, and this used to piss the captains off very much!" Some outright laughter now, someone going to the bar for another round of drinks--

"Well, this one captain was so pissed off that he came back two months later, wanted me to go aboard his boat for dinner. So I went out-- he had one of them gorgeous cooks, you know! Anyway, he gave me so much to drink he said I should stay and they take me home in the morning.

"But when I woke up we were at sea!

"I said, 'Bill,' for that was the captain's name, 'What the heck is goin' on?'

"He said, "I'm gonna take you to look for a wife so you stop pissin' all the captains off when they bring their cooks to Jost!'

"So, which island do you think they took me to, the next one?" Foxy asks the crowd now.

He has them engrossed in the story now, and, even if you've heard it before, just the way he tells it again will be more than just entertainment. It's his story-- and, as they all know now, it's Tessa's story, too.

Someone says, "Cyprus!"

"Not bad," Foxy laughs, strums a little bit. Then he says, "It was Faial, in the Azores."

Giggles and laughter again.

"No wife there. Then they went to Gibraltar, but all the women wrapped up 'cause they were Moslem, I couldn't dig that. Then Palermo, saw all the bullet holes in the walls and came face to face with a Godfather and he say, 'Oh no, boy, you ain't gonna plant no corn in these waters!

"We went to Greece, Corfu, looked for one of Jackie Onassis's cousins on Scorpio, but didn't find one, split to Dubrovnik, did the whole Dalmatian coast, almost got blown ashore on Albania, back to Corfu."

Foxy takes a sip of his Tennant's Stout, strikes a few licks on the guitar, lets the audience get their refills and settle down again.

He then tells them that Bill kicks him off in Corfu. Foxy was being too picky in finding a wife. So Foxy takes a train to Switzerland, Munich, Belgium, Rotterdamn, Leyden, all across Europe--

"Only wooden shoes I saw in Holland were in a glass case for the tourists. Yeah!"

"So I came back to Munich. It was cold. So I flew down to Barcelona, Spain then took a train to Terragona. I'm searching the bars for a wife and who do I run into but the same damn captain! He says, 'Foxy, get your black ass back aboard the boat and we'll keep searchin'.

"We went down the coast of Spain. I met Tessa in Gibraltar, sailed her across the Atlantic to St. Barth's, give her a lobster dinner, two bottles of wine. We had a fine time!

Some sighs from the women at the tables, smiles on the men. It's suddenly quiet.

"Only one lie in the story," Foxy says now.

Some nervous laughs--we're going to hear it now...

"I wasn't shanghaied. No, I went sailing of my own accord with that Bill Bodle on his schooner, and I was looking for a wife."

He picks a bit, searching for a tune.

"And just one regret," Foxy laments, looking back towards the bar at Tessa. "And that was, that it didn't happen twenty years before!"

A load of laughter from tables and benches now, the place suddenly crowded, as though Foxy, that black magnet, had drawn in every tourist on Jost to hear his most famous tale.

And he sings:

Now don't you laugh,
It's no big joke!
It's the reason today Foxy's broke!
Because I am so broke, I could really cry
Because our oldest daughter goes to Lehigh!
On, dee dee day, O dee dee dah...

Someone in the crowd asks what Justine is studying in college. Foxy sits back a bit, strums his guitar, and thanks a few people for the dollars they've been stuffing in his tip jar.

"Well," he says, "she's gonna be an engineer."

Some questioning oohs and aahs-- and one tourist says, "Well, then she can help you around here with the construction...!"

There's always some construction work going on at Foxy's. Today there's a few guys painting tables over on the side of the deck. Also, there are a couple of guys on the roof who occasionally chuck pieces of material off which lands with a crash! There's some sawing and hammering going on, too.

"Yeah," Foxy goes on. "She gonna do the type of engineering where she take fifty dollars here and make it into a hundred dollars over there. Financial engineering, I think they call it."

A bunch more laughing. Justine is actually majoring in

English and Business, Tessa told me.
And Foxy goes into another song:

> Now I hope, you don't get in a rumpus,
> for your next president is coming from Texas!
> And just in case you don't know
> His name is Ross Perot!

Some gasps, some titters, and someone asks Foxy who he thinks will win, really now?

> Well, I'm a-gonna play,
> Right here on my fiddle.
> Ross Perot gonna split it right down the middle!
> It gonna be like this,
> It gonna be all right!
> "Cause he not looking to the left or the right!
> But now that I seem into it,
> I ain't got much push.
> Clinton chop down Perot,
> Now he chop down Bush!
> I tell on lie,
> A bush burn well when it is dry!
> An' this ain't no joke,
> Clinton gonna put Bushy up in smoke!
> Now I want you to go on laughing
> Ever'y body stayin' nice!
> Bush busts Saddam's ass once'
> He could bust it twice!
> Now I ain't gonna shout,
> But only Saddam now can bail Bushy out.
> And, I say to you,

Prepare yourself for Desert Storm Number Two!

He has them pretty well primed now. There are happy faces all around. People, both old and young, are sitting around Foxy's like they are attending a family reunion. They're at ease. Comfortable. And why not? Why shouldn't they be? The harbor is beautiful, its water clear, and the famous Foxy Callwood is entertaining them....

Seeing that everybody's in good spirits, Foxy goes into another song:

> I ask my old lady what I must do
> to make her happy and make love too--
> She say the only thing I really want from you,
> Is a little bitty piece of the big bamboo!
>
> I give that woman a sugar cane,
> The sweet side I did explain.
> She give it back, said it was nice.
> She love the flavor, but not the size!
> Give that woman a banana plant.
> She say, "Hey, honey, it's elegant.
> But let's not let it go to waste,
> It's much too soft to suit my taste!"
> Give that woman a coconut.
> Said to me, "Honey, it's all right, it's still elegant.
> But what good is the nut without the plant?"
>
> She want biggee biggee biggee big bamboo!

The usual afternoon crowd is here. Foxy doing his thing, the tourists shuffling from the bar over to the T-shirt shop and back.

Then a very pretty girl comes in dressed in a tight skirt with long dark hair--a knockout in any sense. The Fox looks over at me. I'm sitting there alone, tape recorder going, camera sitting there impotent-- I'm staring at the girl.

Finally I look at him. He laughs now-- Gotcha!

Meet me tonight in the moonlight,
I tell you a story that's never been told.
I wish I had wings as a angel, over the sea I would fly!
I would fly to the arms of my darling
And there I would stop wondering why?
I wish I was single again
'Cause when I was single, my money still jingle
I wish I was single again!

Foxy asks everyone present where they are from.

Today, they're mostly from Massachusetts. The pretty girl is from Martha's Vineyard. He goes into an impromptu ditty as to why some places are more famous than others, sprinkling the song with allusions to bridges, and then ends it with:

Now listen, I gonna tell you quick
The name of that bridge is Chappaquidick!

General laughter. "Such is life," Fox says. "Such is life!" Then he keeps going--

I was amazed
The family keep their name in the paper
Until these days!
Now I hope you agree with me,
Last big scandal was down there in Mi-ami!
It only fit
They couldn't change
Not one bit!
Now I tell you, I dance in France,

That boy get in trouble every time he drops his pants!

Somebody wants to order another drink--- make that a couple
of them. Others are stuffing dollars in Foxy's tip jar. A
number of cameras appear. There's no bartender, and I'm
about to get behind the counter when Tessa comes around the
corner, "Sorry! Absentee bartender!"
Foxy has the pretty girl right next to him, her relatives
around and clustered behind. I get to snap the picture.

> One thing I do regret.
> You gotta sit there polluting
> With your cigarette!
> If you really know the trick
> You would stop smoking that cancer stick!
> And if you're really into saving the whales,
> I'm begging you to stop smoking them coffin nails!
> So I'm gonna come right down to the point,
> You really gonna smoke,
> You might as well smoke a ... CIGAR!

A whole new group saunters in, They are a bunch of young
guys from the States. They look capable, somehow.
"So," Foxy asks, "Where you boys from?"
"I saw you in a video," one of them says.
Foxy puts his finger to his lips, looking around, "Shhhh!"
"Yeah," the guy goes on. "It was you! That 'Girls of
Penthouse' calendar layout!"
Foxy has the calendar, of course, so he breaks it out.
"Tell me when you see anybody you know in here," he tells
me as I leaf (slowly, now) past the months...my, my, April...
ahh, August! Now, really, November!
But there he is, smack dab in the center of a collage of these
chicks from heaven on the back page...

Later on, Fox told me about the donation the publisher made to the JVDPS. Then some charter boat people came in, and Foxy goes immediately into entertainment mode:

Now skipper, I'm really tellin' no lies,
How come you not wearing your glasses on your eyes?
They down on your chest, like you don't care
Man, you're holding your glasses
Like they was your brassier!
I really really hope, you won't be hurt--
If they were your bra,
They should be under your shirt!

Foxy and the charter people talk about St Thomas a bit. There are lots of changes happening in Charlotte Amalie.

This reminds Foxy of a story. He mentions he recently stopped at the Bridge Bar in Yacht Haven for a drink... and he wasn't in the door five steps before a really gorgeous barmaid comes up to him...

"Now, usually, whenever a young lady see you with your fly open, she say, 'Pardon me, sir, your zipper is down.' But this chick come up to me and say, 'Hey, boy, your garage door is open!'"

"She kindda smile, I think she got something on her mind. So I say to her, 'Honey, when you see that garage door open, did you see that ...BIG ....BLACK....SHINING CADILLAC parked in the garage?'

"She said, 'Hell, no! But I saw a little Volkswagen with two flat tires!'"

Later on that evening, I'm listening to Foxy talking with some of the his local friends who have stopped in for a drink and conversation. At times the West Indian patois is so thick I have difficulty understanding it.

The talk is basically about farming on the island, and planting in particular. Foxy told about the time he had to give up cultivating the big plants up the hill when he'd strained his back.

He'd done this helping a friend unload a stove off a boat out in the harbor. He'd felt some pain then, and had gone to a chiropractor. But somehow the chiropractor had messed one of his ribs, and Foxy started getting weaker and weaker.

He had to let everything go. No doctor could help him, he just continued to get sicker.

Finally, he goes to this herbal doctor, who immediately made some bush tea to revive him. He told Foxy that his flesh was one day away from just falling away from his bones.

And Foxy tells about a dream he had just that same night after seeing the herbal doctor. In the dream he sees himself stepping out of a coffin--

He ended the story with "Dis be true! Foxy lives forever!"

A couple of people come in. They look like they're right off a cruise ship. It's as though they took a wrong turn off Back Street in downtown Charlotte Amalie-- and magically ended up here. They're not exactly sure which rabbit hole they've fallen into. So the man, an elderly gent, in his seventies, asks the closest person, since he can't find Alice, "This is nice here?"

Of course, he asked Foxy.

"No, this is terrible place!"

Everybody laughs, then the elderly gent laughs, his wife laughs-- and they sit down, glad to have found a place to rest.

"Where you folks from?"

They say Florida.

"They still speaking English there?"

"I think so," says the gent, as though maybe he's not even sure anymore. "There is a lot of Spanish spoken, especially in

41

Miami."

"Well," Foxy tells me that Jost and all the Virgins could be Haiti. "We be lucky here," he said. "But we have to work to keep it that way."

More people filter into the bar, some obviously have come for the main attraction-- the man himself. He gets up on his usual perch, one of the big tables with the Iolaire-Imray charts decoupaged on the table tops. Most of the group is from North Carolina, and Foxy goes into a story about a man from Texas visiting that state...

"So this Texan, he riding around the countryside of North Carolina in his big Cadillac, sees this farmer, and asks him how big his farm is.

"'Well,' the farmer tells the Texan, 'if you look up to that ridge yonder (and he points to a far away line of hills), and then to the fence over there, and then the other one that runs along the road, well, mister, that's all mine.'

"Now this North Carolina farmer is very proud of his holdings there, but the Texan isn't out done. He says to the farmer, 'Well, pardner, that's very nice, but it takes me all day just to ride around my ranch back home in Texas.'

"The farmer just stares at him, and then says, 'Yeah, I used to have a truck like that years ago, too...'"

Lots of laughter now. Foxy strums on his guitar a bit. I can tell he's hunting up a ditty-- the folks are content with their drinks for the moment.

Suddenly, Foxy sees a friend of his leaving the harbor in a small boat. He excuses himself, runs over to the bar, and grabs a big conch shell from under it.

He blows on the conch shell; it's distinctive sound booms across the water. You can see the boat slowing down now, then the same sound is heard issuing from the boat. The boat

42

then speeds up again, and in a moment is gone out of the harbor.

Foxy returns to his spot, explaining that he was just making sure that his friend didn't forget the errand he needed done in Tortola.

One of the tourists was quick enough to catch Foxy in the act of blowing on the big conch shell with her camera. I wish I had done so-- for it was a classic shot. A tropical beach, and a handsome island native sounding with his traditional instrument...

Of course, Foxy's has a modern VHF marine radio right behind the bar. He uses it often for business. But he also realizes that there is something magic about a conch shell, and how it epitomizes 'de islands, mon!' to his guests...

So Foxy tells the crowd about his plans for the USA. He figures he can take care of the deficit, unemployment, crime, etc. "Well, I goes to Uncle Bush with my plan, you know. And he likes my idea! I'll get tax incentives, all that stuff. So I'm gonna be heading north soon to start breaking ground on my new project..."

"What's that?" someone asks as Foxy playfully picks at the guitar.

"Well," he says, "there are too many companies leaving America. So, I figure I'm going for the honeymooners. People are still getting married up there-- right?"

Laughter--

"So in my research I finds out that the majority of the white folks go to Niagara Falls. Now, I figure that what is needed is a place for the black folks to go on their honeymoons. So I found the ideal location."

He hits a few chords,someone buys him a Tennant's Stout. Finally, someone asks him where the 'ideal location' is--

"The ideal location, I figure, is this place called Coon Rapids."

Foxy finds out that some of his guests are police officers. He breaks out his honorary hat with the big gold badge on it. The badge is from the Cook County, Illinois, Sheriff's Department. At least one of the police officers currently works out of Chicago.

> Now I do agree,
> I feel I am a police in my society.
> I realize my life is fine,
> I don't want a thing to steal or to hurt mankind!
> Oh dee dee dee, On dee dee dah...

Foxy asks the group, "What is one word that you call a Polack with a five hundred dollar hat?"
A chorus of answers, ranging from 'rich?' to 'poor?'
The Fox just shakes his head. No one ever gets this one--
"Pope," he cries out.

The history of Foxy's Tamarind Bar is a haphazard one. Foxy started it with a woman named Ruthy. Ruthy, if you believe the stories, was essentially a castaway...
"Ruthy was the inspiration to me of the whole of Foxy's-- because I have this little bar on the beach, actually for a Harvest Festival. Supposed to be just for *one* day!"
Foxy had fixed up his place so that from the water it stood out-- even then he was aiming his business towards the water trade. Across the front was emblazoned 'MOM'S BOOTH- - FOXY'S BAR! DRINKS 25 CENTS!'
"Ruthy came up to me and said, 'Why don't you add a little

kitchenette and rent it to me?'"

Ruthy, of course, was Ruthy Carstarphen off the charter yacht *Maverick*, a Brixham trawler. She came in Great Harbour often with her husband Jack and their guests. Her reasons for wanting to team up with Foxy probably will remain with her, for she left soon after the partnership began.

Foxy took Ruthy up on her suggestion, but didn't think it was right to permanently stay on the beach. He leased a spot of ground just in from the beach near the Methodist Church, and began collecting lumber and other materials. His method, however, was slow-- he was still fishing for a living back then, and found whatever he could.

Ruthy wasn't excited about the slow progress, so she opened an account for Foxy at a lumber and hardware store and told him to get building!

"But after a few months, she split," said Foxy. "Whatever happened I don't know, she decided to go, so suddenly I had to do everything myself!"

And so he did-- he cooked, played guitar, and tended bar in between. He learned as he went along, and he learned well. Much of what he learned in those days has since become the bedrock of his business.

"Yes," he says now, "it was because of her coming to me and asking to add on a little addition to my shack-- that's how Foxy's came into being!"

Somebody strolls in and says, "How are ya, today, Foxy?"

He answers, "I'm excellent. But I promise to do better tomorrow."

Taking a Hike

Posted like silent sentinels
all around the town
stand men fixed in ocean reveries.

-- Ishmael, 'Loomings',
from 'Moby Dick' by Herman Melville

Great Harbour is approached from seaward by heading due north. At night, the harbour is usually crowded with anchored boats. Some of these boats only display a dim anchor light, while others are awash with lights. Many of the vessels have parties in progress.

There are usually a couple of mega-yachts anchored in the harbour. Some of these have tenders large enough to ferry dozens of passengers ashore at once. These large mega-yachts can resemble floating cities on the water-- and are often illuminated brightly by their numerous cabin, deck, and flood lights.

This can make the sailing navigator somewhat intimidated during a night approach. The only good thing about these brightly lit floating condos is that they are usually moored smack dab in the entrance to the harbour. The trick is stay as close as you dare while sailing in. Once beyond their blinding lights you'll regain your vision, and be able to see the other vessels anchored closer in.

Some of the anchored vessels may have only a flickering kerosene lamp for an anchor light-- and a few will have no lights at all-- so be extremely cautious while entering Great Harbour at night.

But along the beach itself, once inside the harbour proper, there are quite a few lights. One good beacon is Happy

Laury's. His place appears to be lit up with colored neon. It gives the odd impression of being an old roadside diner. In the morning, one is almost disappointed to discover that Laury's isn't covered with chrome.

One morning I decided to walk over to Little Harbour on Jost's East End. I packed my gear in a backpack and rowed into Foxy's dock. He met me there, wearing a Hard Rock Cafe T-shirt and a big smile.

He guessed from my outfit that I was going hiking. I had a big straw hat, dark sunglasses, backpack-- but the obvious clue was my socks and beat-up Nikes.

"Which direction are you heading, mon?" he asked, looking at the sun which even now was peeking over the eastern ridge of the harbour.

"Thought I'd take that road up there," I said, pointing up the hill.

"Little Harbour not too far," he said, squinting at the sun now. He smiled. "Nice over there-- you'll like it."

"Will you be working this morning?" I figured I'd be back before lunch.

"No," he told me. "We go to church at eleven. But I'll be around later. Have a good hike!"

I set off, climbing up the road out of Great Harbour. The road was dirt for awhile, then there was a stretch of rough concrete. The sun was strong, but I hit a good stride as the road somewhat leveled out along the south side of the island.

St Thomas looked very serene to the southwest. Many of the other islands were mere green shapes in the hot and humid air. Tortola was to the east, Great Thatch and St John to the south. They looked hazy, and yet picture-perfect.

There was almost no breeze. I was glad I wore a big brimmed straw hat. A few boats were underway between the islands. A couple of them had their sails up, but they didn't appear to be moving. Some power vessels were carving long white wakes in the calm water, and I envied the breeze they created for their passengers.

I soon started to sweat profusely-- but I was glad for it, as a slight hangover began leaving me. I had stayed too long in Foxy's the evening before.

Things had began innocently enough. I had a roti for dinner, and talked to Tessa and Foxy for awhile. But they were both tired, and soon went home to their children.

I stayed on. I wanted to talk to some locals, and I did. I quickly got involved in various conversations which lasted well into the wee hours of the morning. Our talk ranged from fishing to boats to goats, and, of course, international politics.

The people of Jost seem genuinely interested in what is happening in the world, especially in the BVI and the United States. There was a lot of talk about the upcoming US presidential election. Their keen interest is partially economic, but they also seem quite amused by all the mud-slinging.

Along the road, as it dipped and curved along the sloping hillside above the rocky coast below, I listened to the sounds of the morning. There were birds flitting in the bush, some baby goats bleating, and the occasional far-off sound of a power boat gliding by. But mostly there was silence.

I came over a slight rise. Sandy Cay was in the distance. The hot sunlight seemed to bathe it in gold. Beyond was Cane Garden Bay on Tortola. The sparkling sea remained as calm as a lake.

I marched up another hill, and then could see Little Harbour. There were more houses in this area, many set off the road with steep, steep driveways. I could hear the occasional sound of people and their domestic animals stirring.

Little Harbour can be intensely beautiful in the morning light. It was on this occasion. It's about half the size of Great Harbour, and faces southeasterly. There were hardly any boats within, and a number of empty moorings were visible.

A sportfishing boat was heading out of the harbour. There was also a trimaran leaving under auxiliary power with limp sails set.

I followed the road down into the harbour. I was in no particular rush-- just taking my time. I passed a few small boats pulled up along the beach at the end of the bay. It gets shallow quick here, and thus has been known since time immemorial as a good careening hole. You can see the water depths quite easily from up on the hill. The dark blue area is deep, while the light green water signals the shallows.

This would certainly be a fine place to 'heave down' a ship and work on its bottom-- something that was especially important in the days before modern anti-fouling paints.

While these thoughts were going through my head, I saw my first person since leaving Great Harbour. He was shirtless-- which seemed only proper this hot Sunday morning. He was lounging close to a skiff as though contemplating some work.

"How's by you?" he called.

I stopped, grateful for the rest. The sweat was now pooling along the belt line at my back. "Good," I said. I noticed he was in the shade. "You're in the right place."

"Yah, mon. The day be long enough!"

I waved, and moved on.

On the other side of Little Harbour the land rises again. I trudged up the grade. At the top, I could see yet another bay. This body of water is known locally as either Manchineel Bay or Long Bay.

Across from where I stood was Little Jost Van Dyke, and behind it, to the northeast more, was Green Cay. I could see the part of Green Cay which was sandy beach. There were a couple of sloops anchored there. I envied them, as I could see some wind on the water close by.

Off to the north, just west of Little Jost, was a barge and tugboat. The barge was being loaded with sand. A pair of payloaders were busily running back and forth between the massive piles of white material that filled up at least ten acres.

I rested for awhile in the shade of a cliff that overshadowed the road that ran down to the sand pit. There was white surf breaking in the cut between Jost and Little Jost. The waves looking perfectly formed as they rolled in from the Atlantic past the jagged rocks of Dim Don Point.

It was comparatively cool here, and I rested awhile longer, thinking of William Thornton's description of sailing into this bay in 1791 in his letter to John Lettsome...

"When I approached, all was calm and still. Thy ancient habitation was in sight. It looked dreary, but the sun broke upon it and enlivened the promontory on which it was situated. I took a sketch of it from the opposite shore on Great Jost Van Dyke, which I have sent thee...

"I am sailing along the channel when nearly opposite to thy house, where the water was only three or four feet deep and perfectly transparent, we observed the bottom variegated in the most rich and beautiful manner that imagination can conceive.

"It was purple in all the variety of shades mixed with various colored shells of rare and valuable species, with numerous Corallines, Sea Eggs, Stars and Fans also abound, and varied branches of white coral form a net to retain everything that can add to the beauty of this submarine garden.

"Fish of various species of the most splendid colors are to be seen playing round these beautiful and variegated prostricitions; and every stroke of the oar gave such new appearances that the whole seemed to contain an endless and enchanting variety."

I remembered the print of a painting of Little Jost that Tessa had on display in her shop back at Foxy's. It shows Edward Lettsome's mansion sitting atop the island's highest point.

There was nothing there now, and Thornton also mentions that the building was almost gone when he'd visited some two hundred years ago. He does mention the palm trees and the big tamarinds, which seem now to have taken over the island.

I went down the steep road to the sand operation, passing the big dredge that rested back near the mangroves. There were lengths of big black plastic pipe, a construction shack and a few trucks. The only sound came from the payloaders as I walked over the blindingly white coral sand, threading my way in between piles of sand in varying states of gradation.

Some of the piles were quite rough. There were chunks of coral as large as my fist in some; hence graded down to the finest sand, almost powderlike.

I passed by a large grader that was fed by a conveyor belt. It wasn't running today. I moved on along the beach, seeking the surf between the islands.

I couldn't get close enough to the waves, though I could see that the bottom was hard. The seas developed a nice curl as they came ashore though, forming tubes as they rolled in. One could probably have some fun here, provided they wore a Kevlar-reinforced wet suit.

Singular mangrove stalks stuck out of the water in places. They looked strange, and somehow their stalks and leaves reminded me of flamingo birds.

The larger mass of the plants kept me from getting any nearer the surf, though I ventured into the thicket for awhile. There was an interesting pile of rocks facing the smaller island I would have liked to have made it to-- Dim Don Point. The name itself was intriguing. But after fighting the tangled roots and branches for a few steps I remembered that I had a boat and a stout dinghy back in Great Harbour.

Thornton mentions that the slaves had no problem wading the shallows between Jost and Lettsome's Island. I wasn't going to attempt it.

51

Over on Little Jost there was a copse of palms, with a single building situated amongst them. It looked like a perfect place for a beach bar, and in fact had once been Tony and Jackie Snell's 'Last Resort' before they moved their operation to Bellamy Cay off the eastern end of Tortola.

The building is currently the home of Beverly Washburn. She is the manager of Foxy's kitchen/restaurant concession. She shares the place with her daughter, grandchild, and her husband Oraldo. There are only four of them on the whole island now.

I recalled the night before meeting a guy named Nippi of Little Harbour. He told me that his family currently owns half of Little Jost. Quite a change from the 160 or so slaves and overseers who inhabited the island in the early eighteenth century.

Big Jost supported a population of over five hundred back then, all involved in sugar cane production. But by the 1790's the sugar estates of Jost were mostly abandoned, and the land mainly turned over to cotton production.

An interesting thought came to mind. It takes a ton of sugar cane to make thirty gallons of rum. I wondered how much cotton it takes to make a gross of T-shirts.

I was pretty parched by now, and so I labored back up the hill. This stretch of road was paved in the same manner as earlier sections-- that is to say, very roughly. It was not poured this way; the rough trowel work appeared intentional.

I imagine this facilitates traction, especially when it's wet. I know that on St. John-- where the roads were recently covered in black asphalt-- the surfaces can be quite slick. And even when the roads are dry, a sedately driven car will often 'burn rubber' while climbing the hairpin turns.

There are a number of homes here on the east end of the island. Many are painted in the West Indian style, pastel blues and pinks, yellows and pale reds, the trim and shutters different colors from the main structure. Many of the porches are decorated with gingerbread.

Foxy spent much of his youth in this area. He still owns a house here, which he purchased from an uncle. The land came to him from his mother's side-- the Blyden's. They were once a big family on Jost. Most of the former residents of this area either farmed or fished for a living.

Then I met a young lad on the road. He was carrying a small tape deck, and had earphones dangling around his neck. Since he wasn't yet 'tuned in,' as it were, I asked him where I could get a cold drink. We were standing on the hill looking north, and down into the harbour itself.

He pointed out a series of low buildings down on the shore opposite. "That be Harris', there," he said, "the one with the red sign. They be open."

We walked along together, after I'd thanked him. Then he turned into a yard and towards a building that appeared church-like. The walls were stark white and shuttered.

Maybe he was the organist for the morning service-- the tape deck his back up? These people do place a lot of value on their community religious involvement. It *was* Sunday, after all.

But I was looking for a cold beer and a hamburger. I followed the road down again, past the man I'd seen earlier. He was still there, under the tree alongside his vessel.

He had someone with him this time, and they were discussing St. Thomas. "You can get anything you want, St. Thomas," his friend was saying, repeating it over again as I sauntered by, waving in greeting. I pondered this as I found the turn off to Harris' Place. Saint Tee was probably Mecca to the young folks here, just as in my day Manhattan was the place to go when you lived in the in the hinterlands of suburban Long Island.

"You can get anything you want-- at Alice's Restaurant... 'cepting Alice..." I sang as I went along.

53

I never made it to Harris' Place. There was a yellow building along the way, and a jovial rotund figure beckoned me inside.

It was Sidney Hendricks, the owner of the Peace and Love Cafe. He was shirtless, wore a billed cap, and claimed to be open for business. He had cold beer, hamburgers, lobster, or anything else I might need. I immediately decided to rest awhile, and refuel.

He also had a concrete dock with seven feet of depth in front of his restaurant. We had quite a conversation as I poured down a few Amstel Lights. Sidney was naturally loquacious, and he told me a lot about the area, the people who lived close by, and about his plans for a New Year's Eve celebration like they have over in Great Harbour.

I asked him what he thought of the Jost Van Dyke Preservation Society, and he was whole-heartedly for it. He also commented that he rarely leaves Jost if he can help it.

While Sidney wasn't into traveling far away from his home, he appreciated the fact that Foxy Callwood had the experience of traveling and seeing how things were in the rest of the world. He thought Foxy would be a great politician, and meant it quite differently than a lot of us might.

Sidney felt that any more development on Jost would just cause the smaller businesses like his own to be pushed out. This was a sentiment I heard repeated many times on Jost.

He said, "People don't *hear* you other places-- they just pass you by, try to tell *you* what's best for you. They don't know... they *can't* know."

I asked him about the moorings that dotted Little Harbour. Sidney told me that most of them were owned by Moor Secure, a Tortola based operation. But he still had three of his own, though he used to have nine. Visiting boaters could pick up a mooring for the night free of charge if they had dinner at his place.

Across the harbour was Sidney's father's house, which he pointed out to me. The house was right next to Abe's By the Sea, another watering hole. Loquacious as ever, Sidney told me he had ten children, scattered all over now. One of them was a policeman in Cruz Bay on St. John.

Somehow we got on the subject of pirate treasure. Sidney told me an intriguing story about finding some silver and gold coins and a few pieces of jewelry. All on an island "far away, where it takes three days just to get to where the treasure is."

He also mentioned something about attack dogs, so I imagine the property might be privately owned...

But the most interesting part of his story, at least for me, was when he mentioned the fact that there was a faded outline of a ship which was scratched into a wall close to where he found the coins...

It was obviously a very old drawing, and Sidney seemed to think that remaining part of the treasure is probably <u>behind</u> the ship somewhere...

Ah, yes! I love conversations like that. Enigmatic enough to pass the time, and interesting enough to stir the blood. I mean, what are we here for if not to make our fortunes?

But, of course, island treasure is not always in the form of gold or silver. Foxy and Sidney have discovered their 'fortune' is all around him-- in the natural beauty of Jost.

Little Harbour also boasts Harris Jones' Place. It's right alongside Sidney's Peace and Love Bar and Restaurant. There's a small grocery here also. Behind Harris' is his daughter Tula's campground-- another place to stop for the weary camper without benefit of craft.

Jost Van Dyke takes on another perspective from the top of MacJohnny Hill, the highest point on the island. I found the trail with the help of Jemilla, Foxy's daughter. It begins right off the road beyond the laundry near the natural spring that feeds Great Harbour.

Happy Laury Chinnery had mentioned the trail to me that morning. He said there was plenty of Guinea grass up on the hillside, the long stemmed variety that herbivores like. Laury also mentioned that people used to fill their mattresses with the grass. He told me there was once so much "you could go up there and roll around in it!"

That sounded like fun. Luckily, there was no sun on this Friday morning. Some clouds had moved in from the south. It was a good day for a hike. I had socks, and my Nikes. What more did I need?

Actually, the path is not much more than a goat trail. But it is easy enough to follow-- at least for a bit. Walking amid the rocks in the tall grass is very relaxing and peaceful. It reminded me of hiking the West Virginian hillsides of my youth.

Halfway up the hill is a truly outstanding outcrop of rocks. Along the way are numerous fences-- barbed, chainlink, and chicken wire. In places they are pushed down for easy access. The path is used, obviously, by more than goats. There's the odd beer bottle, and other humanoid debris.

And then there's the caves. Along the way are big rocks with hollowed out places where... well, one could *hide out* in some of these declivities. The kid in me (and he ain't very deep down, folks) would have liked to loaf the day away in some of these places. You know, playing cowboys and Indians, or Jew and Arab-- whatever.

Anyway, I arrived at the prominent set of rocks which overlook Great Harbour. There is a natural *seat* at the top-- a perfect spot to lay back and admire the view.

All of the 'town' of Great Harbour is visible below. You can see the shoreline businesses and Custom's house-- the fire station, ice plant, school, and clinic-- even the roads going over to White Bay and Little Harbour.

It reminded me a bit of Drake's Seat over on St. Thomas-- but without the noisy traffic, those obnoxious T-shirt vendors, and that pushy ("Wanna-take-my-picture?") guy with the donkey who wears a hat.

There are a few tethered goats along the way. These animals are, obviously, privately owned. In fact, *all* goats and sheep on Jost *belong* to people.

Large herds of cattle used to roam these hills until fairly recently. Foxy's father owned a number of them. Their numbers rapidly diminished when the USDA changed its importation rules on cattle-- and suddenly the USVI wasn't a market for BVI beef any more.

And, here on Jost Van Dyke, the *land* itself is privately owned. I was, actually, trespassing on private property. This is *not* government property nor Territorial Park; it's private. So it is not a bad idea to ask permission before hiking the area. The answer will probably be, "No problem, mon!"

Of course, if anyone asks you to leave the area for any reason, do so immediately. (Foxy later told me that there is still some 'Crown Land' on Jost-- which hopefully will be set aside in its natural state in conjunction with the Jost Van Dyke Preservation Society.)

I next came across the ruins of a small house. It was tucked in amongst a copse of tamarind trees. There were still some rusted bedsprings inside. It was a standard West Indian 12 x 15 foot structure. It probably once had a thatched roof.

The thought that this solitary house had once been someone's happy home-- filled with the rich sounds of life and love and laughter-- intrigued me. It's inhabitants might have lived out their final days on those ancient iron springs.

It was a fine and private place.

Further along, I came across another spot where the chainlink had been pushed down. Once through, I found myself on a rocky trail which ran east and west.

Laury had mentioned to me that there was a trail running all the way from Little Harbour. I assumed this was it. It wasn't a particularly wide path, but could have served as a decent donkey trail-- suitable for transporting sugar cane or cotton from one estate to another. Foxy mentioned that as a 'young man' he traveled such a road with his own donkey from one end of Jost to the other.

I followed the trail westward. It soon took a sharp turn. The rock formation at the corner of the turn was obviously manmade. There was also a wall a few feet high. I could now see the top, and pressed onward.

A word, here, to the intrepid hiker. Long pants should be worn, as the going gets, well, *goatier*. There's plenty of the 'catch 'n keep' and spiky cactus along the way.

Finally, I reached the top.

We're up over a thousand feet here and the Atlantic stretches out before you all the way to Bermuda and Newfoundland to the north. To the west, that furthest smudge is Puerto Rico. St. Croix is visible to the south, over the top of St. John. East lies the north coast of Tortola, and beyond that is Guana island, the Camanoe's, and the heights of Virgin Gorda. Even further on are the shoals of Anegada.

At my feet is a surveying mark-- Her Majesty's Hydrographic Department's Triangular Station's Marker #31442. A few feet (and a rock or two) to the south is a US Coast and Geodetic Survey Marker. For once in my life, I know *exactly* where I am!

There's sea grape growing up here, and, low and behold, an ancient mahogany tree. A humming bird is darting about the sea grape. Also some, alas, signs of 'civilization'. An empty soda can, a faded candy wrapper, and a spot where someone had to scratch 7-28-1992. (What lengths we mortals go to achieve our brief attempt at immortality!)

Well, some of us hope just to stay in print...

What is really interesting here is the view of the north coast. It is very steep, with rocky cliffs. And in the Atlantic Ocean, directly out from the rocky shore of Jost, stretch long white lines of sea foam into the dark blue sea. They look like boat wakes-- and at the time I assumed there must be rocks or something below the surface to make the water froth like this. However, I can't discern anything from the top. (A later perusal of the chart shows nothing to cause such an effect.) These stretches of white water seem to be stationary. Yet I can clearly see the movement of the ocean swells beyond them. One line of froth is peculiarly long, stretching out from the shore a good quarter mile.

I watch this phenomena for at least twenty minutes. I'm both puzzled and intrigued. Foxy told me later these lines are caused by currents that run out from the island. Binoculars would have been helpful-- but mine were aboard my boat, safely stowed away.

Today, the air up here is fairly dead. It feels like it wouldn't support a butterfly. The sky is overcast, and for that I am grateful.

I study the ridges and hollows below to see if I can spot any trails. I see some possibilities, but it is difficult to tell. From this lofty perch, the island appears very virgin-like indeed.

I observed some of the places around Jost with the interesting names, such as Dim Don Point, Pull and Be Damn, Georgy Hole, and Cherry Ghut Bay. There was Man-o-War Hill, Roach Hill and, below it, far to the east, Boo Point.

Immediately below me is On The Cay Hollow Point. Dog Point is just to the east, where that one long white 'wake' seems to emanate from. There's Pulpit Rock near the west end, and a place called Cotton Ground in the center of the island. Also there's Skeleton Land to the east. But Foxy tells me the name 'Skeleton' is really <u>Skelton</u>, and is named after an original settler. I can also just make out the entrance to Manchineel Bay, which separates Little Jost from the main island.

On the way down I discovered numerous pieces of thick glass. They appeared to have once been pieces of large containers of some type. The pieces which lay exposed to the sun were almost black, but similar chunks under rocks were clear. It appeared to be the same glass-- with similar markings and the same thickness. I saved a chunk with a spout. It's an inch and a quarter in diameter, and quite rough-hewn. I'm fairly sure it wasn't manufactured by Annheuser-Busch.

Then I regained the old track. There were plenty of loose and tethered goats in the area. Quite a few of these goats were behind a fence-like contraption made of old fish-and-volley-ball netting.

There were lots of natural declivities in the big boulders, as though worn through by the rain. I also spotted some schist-like material in one spot. It might have been quartz.

Later that same day, as I ate a tasty mutton stew for lunch at Foxy's (I had spotted Virginia the cook cutting the meat earlier, and couldn't resist) a local fellow asked me about my hike.

His name is Godwin, and he sported a nasty gash directly in the center of his forehead. He seemed particularly concerned about the goats.

It turns out they are <u>his</u> goats up there on the hill. And that same morning, while attempting to corral a particularly frisky one, the goat had somehow managed to toss Godwin head first in a mess of barbed wire. Hence the cut between his eyes.

He was concerned about how many goats had escaped his

netting arrangement along the former 'track' up the mountain there. Bleeding profusely, and not sure just how badly he was hurt, he had quickly come down to the clinic.

He was feeling better now, and was glad to hear the goats were still in his makeshift pen. He'd intended to bring them to market but fate had given the goats another day of reprieve.

Godwin admitted that keeping the goats wasn't particularly fun, but had its advantages. "If hard time come-- if push come to push-- you know you can go up *there* (the mountain)-- and get something for *here* (he rubbed his belly)."

I liked Godwin. He wears a black beret, and is muscular in stature. He makes his own way, as most do on Jost.

He's an interesting fellow, and full of surprises. On the night I had attempted to drink all the rum at Foxy's he'd recited a long story to me-- all in rhyme.

I can remember the actual moment of his recital quite distinctly. Godwin seemed very impressive with his black beret and ferocious (it seemed at the time) demeanor. But the actual words he spoke or what the poem was about-- well, I'm afraid all the rot-gut rum swirling in my brain prevented its retention.

"More obscene than anything is inertia."
-- Henry Miller

I learned at the BVI Folk Museum in Roadtown that the last house built by the wattle and daub construction method was (supposedly) on Jost Van Dyke. I asked Happy Laury about it, but he seemed fairly certain it had been knocked down some time ago.

We were looking out at the harbour during this conversation, and I wondered aloud about how quickly things changed--

from islands to boats. I then asked Laury what he thought about Foxy's Jost Van Dyke Preservation Society.

"I think it's a good thing. I go along with him (Foxy) all the way," he said. "This is a very happy place here. We would all like to keep it that way."

He went on to say that large-scale development would take a long time anyway-- since most of the land is still family-owned, and the families are scattered all over. It's a complicated process to get clear title to a big tract. This is a familiar story, especially on a tiny island like Jost where almost everyone is inter-related.

But Laury is fairly content with his lot in life, as are most of the other people on Jost. They all seem to have 'enough' to get by, though they continue to expand and develop their businesses.

Laury had made changes since I'd last visited his place. He'd added an ice cream parlour in the front corner of the building. He still has the only pool table on Jost Van Dyke. Laury has been in business for a long time, having started out with the first snack bar on the beach. He took over his current location, the old M&M Bar, a few years ago.

Laury looks a lot younger than his years-- something he takes bets on from unwary tourists. If they get within three years, Laury buys the bar drinks. Otherwise, they do.

He has a son who teaches school on St. John, and three married daughters who have moved away. He seems to regret that his children don't live on Jost, but he mentioned proudly that his mother was still on the island and lived just behind the ice house.

I mentioned I'd read in the museum that Jost had once been famous all over the Caribbean for its large calabashes. This brought out the frustrated farmer in Laury. (Many of the older people on Jost have a deep love of farming.) He eagerly regaled me with stories on how well things grew on the island, especially on the north side. There were many hollows there in which bananas, mangoes, breadfruit, limes, pineapple, and plantains grew. Yams, cassava, sweet potatoes and corn were all cultivated at one time, he said. But these days, few people farmed.

I mentioned the dearth of water elsewhere in the Virgins. Laury said water was not a problem on Jost. They had their own sweetwater spring.

"I don't know where it comes from," he said, giving me a glass. "But it's good water."

I usually make it a rule to never drink the local water, no matter *where* I am, but I couldn't bring myself to refuse Laury. And the water was good. (Later, I realized I'd passed right by the concrete casement which contained the spring. It was near the beginning of path which Jemilla Callwood had called Spring Mountain.)

Walking the beach, I went by Ali Baba's and the Club Paradise, both closed this early in the day. Christine's Bakery was open. It was hard to pass by with such sweet bakery smells wafting down the beach!

As I stood in line behind some cruising folk at Christine's, I noticed the wind had gone more to the south. Great Harbour was still calm, though. All the boats were facing straight out, as though part of an armada massed for an attack on St. John.

The harbour was fairly full, but, as Laury had observed, not many people were ashore. There was some unusual weather in the offing. I could feel it in the air. Despite the fact the wind was light, there was a big north swell running. Anchorages like Cane Garden Bay were already getting uncomfortable.

I got up to the window at Christine's, and peered in through the bakery's glass case. The big chocolate cookies looked delicious, so I got two. They didn't last long.

There's a Methodist Church in Great Harbour. It holds services at 11 on Sunday mornings. Everyone on Jost used to attend this church, Foxy told me, until a Church of God opened up on the east end. It has a more fundamentalist bent, one that required utter devotion both spiritually and financially. It has caused a lot of problems out that way, he said.

This reminded me of one of Foxy's jokes. "Jimmy Swaggart is putting out a new magazine, and it's gonna be on the newsstand soon. He's gonna call it... *Repenthouse!*"

Both the school and the clinic on Jost are set back from the beach. Tessa had said there were 18 students currently attending school. One of the main factors behind Justine's being able to attend Lehigh University was the scholarship program offered to outstanding students from Jost Van Dyke by the BVI government.

On the far west end of the beach in Great Harbour is Rudy's Mariner Inn. This is the only guest house facility in Great Harbour. It has five rooms, each with its own kitchenette. Along with the bar and restaurant, Rudy's has the only other grocery store on Jost, the other being over in Little Harbour.

And his prices aren't that bad. Leroy, Rudy's son, was holding down the fort this not-so-busy morning. (I don't think a single person passed in the half hour I was there.) He told me the Irish cheddar cheese was four bucks a pound. There was a nice big wheel of it sitting on the counter, and I happen to favor it. But the other edibles weren't out of line-- hell, rum at less than four dollars a bottle ain't bad no matter where you are!

David, Rudy's Inn manager, quoted me room prices at $75.00 per night during the summer, and $125 during season. He said they were booked six to seven months in advance. The only other rooms available on Jost were around the corner at White Bay. But that's another operation entirely, and priced accordingly.

I asked Leroy what he thought of Jost. He's sixteen, and goes to high school in Red Hook on St. Thomas. "Well," he told me, "I just come here to relax, and, of course, to *paah-tee!*"

The life of a live-aboard cruising sailor is sometimes a difficult one. Take last Friday night for example. It was squally. The wind blew like crazy for awhile, then suddenly dropped. All the boats anchored in Great Harbour were tugging on their anchor rodes like kids around the Maypole. It rained for awhile, and then got all sticky and still.

The stars were bright in the night sky. They looked close enough to touch. Orion was riding above the big hill to the east, and Cassiopeia was over towards the northwest.

Because of a wind shift, I realized I might be in too close to the beach. I checked my depth. There was only a couple of feet under my keel. The lack of depth made me nervous. I decided that discretion was the better part of valor-- and decided to do something about it. After all, if a similar blow to the one which came through Roadtown Harbor the other morning hits us, well, things could get *dicey*.

I decided to set out a third hook. It is a big folding fisherman anchor which I'd gaffed from somewhere. It was snuggled up alongside a couple of lifeline stantions on the forward deck, and I got the dinghy ready to deploy it.

There was still boat traffic in the harbor, despite it being 2:30 on a Saturday morning. The dance band had quit playing at Foxy's quite some time ago, but there was still some drunk wailing on the dock. "Dulcinea! Dulcinea! I'm on the dock! Commmme geeeet meeeeee!"

A dink loaded with people went by. Its occupants were giggling and singing some ditty as they wallowed along. I wondered if it was the crew of the Dulcinea on their way to pick up their lost friend.

My fisherman anchor weighs sixty pounds. I humped it carefully into the bottom of my dinghy from the forward deck. The pins holding the shanks and flukes in place had to be *persuaded* to move. It took time. I'm glad I was not doing this as my vessel dragged down on some lawyer's yacht.

I rowed quietly to seaward. The anchorline was paying out nicely when I heard from a near-by vessel, "Hey, she's got no clothes on!"

There was a startled shriek or two, then a lot of laughter. Someone shined a spotlight from one boat to another. That produced even more laughter...

I dumped my anchor overboard, and felt good about having it down. Another unlit dinghy loaded with people went by, and this one was moving pretty fast. The spotlight caught this crew harshly-- they were tight-lipped and mean-looking, as though they were very tired and/or drunk.

There were more wild shrieks from a Beneteau anchored off my starboard side-- they'd gotten into the harbor late, and were making up for lost time.

A women was screeching the name "Jackie" over and over again from across the harbor, and a big Grand Banks nearby cranked up the volume on their stereo as if they'd <u>had</u> it with all this noise...

I crawled back into my warm bunk. Just as I drifted off to sleep, I heard the guy on the end of Foxy's dock still yelling weakly... "Come get mee-e-e-e..."

Saturday morning and I'm feeling *groovy*, as we used to say a thousand years ago.

I row into the dock, happy I had managed to get the big hook over the night before. It blew fairly hard till early in the morning, and I had been as close to the bottom as I wanted to get.

I noticed that Wendell, one of Foxy's sons, has got his boat in the water. He'd been doing fiberglass work on it for the past week. It's blue now, and he's got a borrowed 75 horse on the transom. It'll be enough to get him over to St. Thomas, where he has a 90 hp Mercury waiting.

Of course, he has to do a little work on *this* engine first. Just to get it *running*, you understand...

But he's also working the bar at Foxy's today.

Hey, *no problem*, I tell Wendell. *I* can tend bar. I used to own one...

So I'm behind the bar when Foxy rolls in.

There are already some tourists in the bar, gawking at this and that. Each has a drink in their hand made by yours truly. Painkillers, Pina Coladas, and White Russians-- I know 'em all.

The Fox breaks out his guitar and goes to work.

A big guy comes over to me, and starts shooting the breeze about how good the tool business is in St. Croix.

A local guy comes in, and asks if I got a pair of pliers. I point out to the dock where Wendell is working on his outboard, but the guy tells me it was Wendell who just sent him.

Wendell is attempting to remove a certain type of retaining ring which is commonly known as a Jesus clip.

Suddenly, the tool guy is interested. He engages the local fellow in a wide ranging discussion about tools in general. While doing so, he orders another Painkiller for himself, his wife, his buddy, his buddy's wife, and, oh yes, a Pina Colada for the local guy...

I wonder if one of the women is named "Jackie"...

67

An elderly couple stroll in, and ask for a Miller Lite. I give them an Amstel, and they don't complain.

A couple of West Indian customers stop in, and are surprised to see someone they don't know behind the bar. They order Heinekens. Godwin comes by and says, "Your count be good, man!"

Say what?

He laughs as I search around behind the bar for ice, matches, cups, and various mixers-- people are really crowding in the place now. The ferry just arrived, and the cruisers are in off their boats, the sun is up and cooking...

"The goats, man," Godwin says. "I didn't lose a one."

Yeah, right. The 'volleyball net' pen.

"Great," I say. I ask him when and how he's going to take the goats to market. Does he take the ferry with them?

"Hell," he says. "I take eight or nine at a time right there in the Whaler." He points down the dock.

I know his Whaler. It's not a big one. It must be quite a sight, Godwin and his goats.

Then a woman comes up to the bar. There is a look of concern on her face. I know that look. It's trouble.

She says, "Somebody might want to take a plunger..."

Her eyes aren't steady on mine, and I know she's uncomfortable just telling me this.

"In the ladies head, 'mam?" I say.

"Uh-uh," she nods, glad that I understand. "there was some paper in the toilet and I tried to flush it but it's not flushing and ...."

It's all right. Her name was Doris or Dolly or Bunny, and it was only 10:30 in the morning-- and she was on her third or fourth Painkiller, and ...

I sent her over to Pam in Foxy's T-shirt and *chotchka* shop. At least Pam will know where to find the goddamn plunger. I was lucky to find the top to the blender! This is not your

68

average beer-and-a-shot bar, that's for sure.

Jemilla, Christian, and a friend came in for sodas, and hang out for a bit They perch on the barstools watching me-- they're having a good old time. I'm cheap entertainment.

Christian asks me if I saw him do a flip before. I did, out on the beach earlier. He is sporting a new Simpson-style haircut, and is the envy of all the youngsters on Jost. Jemilla asks if I found the path to the mountain, and I thank her for her help. They finally lose interest, and take off.

Foxy has the audience enthralled, as usual. "You know how Jost Van Dyke gets its name?" he asks the crowd.

A series of "no's..."

"Well," he begins, "it seems there was this Dutch captain, and he come upon this island here. Now, it didn't look like anything was here at all. So what do you think he did?"

Of course, rising to the bait, there are a couple of off-beat answers...

"Well, I tell you," Foxy goes on. "his ship had been at sea for a *long* time, you know. And in those days, they din't have no good looking cooks like they do now on the charter boats."

Some scattered laughter now...

"So, this captain, he figure he send one man ashore to check it out. And what do you think he found?"

"Treasure," somebody says.

"What?" an easily exasperated woman wants to know.

So Foxy strums a bit, then says, "These Dutch pirates had everything they needed, you know-- they got all the treasure already, got food, got water from the other islands. They only missing one thing..."

"What did the guy on shore find?" someone asks.

Foxy stares in his direction and says, "Well, he finally come back to the beach-- right over there, you know... and he's all scratched up. His face is a terrible mess, his clothes are torn... no, he don't look so good..."

69

"What *happened*?" the one lady wants to know. I look her over, wondering if *her* name is Bunny.

Foxy laughs now, shaking his head. "Well, I'm going to tell you. The captain sees his man on the beach, and he yells out, "Are there any women on the island?' For *that's* what they were looking for, you know."

He picks a few chords on the guitar. "And what do you think the man on shore yelled back?"

No answers...

"Oh, *jost vun dyke*, Captain!"

The man who needed the special tool comes back in looking for the guy who had some small pliers. I don't know what happened to him. But then <u>his</u> buddy shows up, and they ask me if they can use my dinghy to go out to their boat. I say sure, but they have to row...

...well, they decide they'll walk all the way back down to the government dock and take their own outboard-powered dink.

Someone wants food, but the kitchen isn't open until dinner. I pour a few more Painkillers, and make someone another rum drink.

A young guy comes in with a pretty girl. He asks Foxy if he can play his guitar. Fox hands it over, and the kid gets into some old Neil Young stuff. Pretty good, actually. The girl is beaming at him. I'm envious-- of a lot of things.

Foxy slides by, going out the bar by the kitchen. "Bartender," he says, "See ya later. Taking a break..."

Wendell comes back in. He got the engine running, but not great. But it shouldn't be a problem, really. It should get him there, maybe.

I decide to check out White Bay. However, I notice that the sky is covered with big grey clouds. The wind is out of the south again. It feels like rain. But it's not too far to where I want to go-- just over the hill to the west. Still, I don't want to get soaked.

I put my tape recorder inside a plastic bag, and head out. A few big drops come down, but that's about it. The wind had picked up, though, and I keep a steady eye on my boat as I walk up the hill. I can see all of Great Harbour from here, and can even hear the voices of the folks on a big trimaran as it comes sailing in. They're obviously having fun, all of 'em laughing and singing.

I'm over the other side now, heading down to White Bay. I can see Black Point, where the road becomes a goat path and then the beach.

There's a new building on the beach with 'White Bay Camp Ground' nicely lettered on the sign. It's still obviously in the building process. There are pieces of material and stuff neatly piled about. I meet Ivan Chinnery, who is doing the actual work. He owns the campground with his sister-in-law, Gertrude Coakley.

Ivan has already cleared three campsites, and plans to have eight or nine done by season. He's set up a barbecue area where folks can congregate while cooking their meals.

The campsites, from what he showed me, will be quite private from each other. There will be both open platforms and permanent tent arrangements. The main building on the beachfront will have a small snack bar, bathrooms, and a camping supply operation.

Ivan confides in me that he really considers himself a simple farmer-- and all this construction work is new to him. Despite this, he appears to be doing a professional job. He has situated the barbecue area nicely, and the campsite placements indicate a real knack for working within the natural environment. It was already a comfortable place.

We talk about Foxy and the Preservation Society. Ivan is behind the goals of the Society. "We expect that we will grow (the island in general), but at the minimum."

The wind was blowing a bit now, out of the southwest-- something unusual here. As Ivan Chinnery told me, "When we see southwester coming, then we know-- squalls, wind, stuff like that."

Ivan had a boat that was coming dangerously close to the beach as the wind increased. He was anxious to get back to Great Harbour, and I couldn't blame him.

Before he left, Ivan told me that he was famous for the pineapples and mangos he grew. His real love is farming-- but opportunities are opportunities. He was building the White Bay Camp Ground for his future, and the future of his family.

Later on, I met Ivan again at Foxy's. He invited me to see his plantings up the mountain. I was particularly impressed with his pineapples.

The walk up the beach to White Bay's Sandcastle was interesting. The wind was directly onshore as I mentioned; the sky overcast. I enjoyed clambering over the rocks at Black Point.

Except for the temperature, I could have been traversing a beach in northern California... or Maine... or the eastern end of Long Island.

I was taken by surprise by a young guy running barefoot over the rocks with a little yellow dog at his heels. He came up over a rise so suddenly he was startled like a wild animal. He seemed out of sorts, as though he didn't know just where to go, now.

I've been that way myself.

His dog reminded me of my own Labrador retriever who was probably being hopelessly spoiled, pampered and feted some 1400 miles north of here.

And that reminded me of Foxy's dog-- and how everything in Foxy's world end up in one of his songs or jokes.

"Can anyone tell me what type of dog that is, laying over there underneath the table," Foxy asks his audience.

Somebody says, "Labrador..!"

Foxy shakes his head. "No, that's a pure bred *island* dog. And you know why?"

No one does. There's consternation in the peanut gallery.

"There are three characteristics of an island dog. He's black, lays around on his ass all day, and he doan know who is father is!"

The Sandcastle, like their brochure says, is not for everyone. And White Bay is physically nothing like Great Harbour. There is no real harbour here, just a small anchorage tucked between a shallow reef and the shore.

The Sandcastle and its Soggy Dollar bar are the extent of 'civilization' here. Gertrude Coakley is reported to have a little beach bar further west along the beach from the Soggy Dollar, but I found no evidence of it. There are a few private homes tucked away here and there, and, as mentioned, Ivan Chinnery's White Bay Camp Ground down the beach.

But that's about it. The only other place on Jost to rent a roof for the night is Rudy's Mariner Inn.

White Bay has two small reefs which can be ducked behind, making it an acceptable anchorage in settled weather. But you're still exposed to any south weather.

The one afternoon I spent there the wind was out of the southwest. This is rare. I watched a pair of charter boats from the Moorings 'hobbyhorsing' so much that one would have to be *extremely* nimble just to climb aboard.

Of course, things always *look* more intimidating from the beach, don't they?

There were two charter groups ashore the day I visited. The bareboaters, many of whom looked like retirees, decided to have lunch ashore at the Sandcastle.

The other group was a bit younger. Their female captain was a long-haired blond. She was in her twenties, and dressed for action in a blue and white bikini.

After her party had a drink, she herded them back down the beach to the inflatable. She held it in place in the surf as they literally 'rolled' aboard. It looked like fun. I didn't get to watch them climb aboard their big Beneteau sloop, but that was probably a good show too.

Darrell, the current owner of the Sandcastle, offered to show me around. The business is for sale, and has already had a few nibbles. There was the bar, the restaurant, a small boutique, and four cottages-- all on an acre and a third. Asking price is in the high six figures.

It's truly a beautiful spot. The beach is... just perfect in every detail. There's a feeling of splendid isolation. The sounds of the surf, sea, and wind is constant-- and utterly relaxing.

A few charter boats can anchor off the beach, but only a half dozen fill the small anchorage behind the reef.

Like the brochure says, "The principal activity at the Sandcastle is.... nothing."

Sandcastle is low-key, but high class. Darrell stressed that the cuisine is superior, and the service excellent. They make everything possible on the premises, and are especially noted for their desserts and baked goods.

He tries to maintain a certain genteel level of excellence, and feels that he has succeeded. The rates, at $295 a couple during season, reflect this.

I'll confirm the Heineken is nice and cold.

Darrell is sorry to have to offer the place for sale, but he has pressing family business back in the States. He likes it here in the BVI, and particularly on Jost, where, he says, "There is no crime! No theft!"

The open bar and kitchen is testimony to that. There are no doors or windows to lock.

There's also no electric power as yet. They use candlelight and twelve volt lights mostly-- the 12kw generator is just for emergencies, according to Darrell.

The decor in the cottages is nice, and the design of the grounds is tasteful. The boutique is filled with hand-painted and appliqued goods made by Darrell's significant other, Kay.

It seems a well-run, quiet operation-- and one which might be perfect for a well-off, reflective guest in search of quiet relaxation..

Ambiance is the key word at Sandcastle. And this is something that it, and all of Jost, has in abundance.

On the hike back to Great Harbour, I noted where the electrical transformers ended. It was quite a distance up the beach from Sandcastle, and also from the White Bay Camp Grounds.

I recalled a few days ago in Foxy's when a tourist who hadn't been on Jost for some time chided Foxy about the bar now having electricity. The tourist remembered Foxy as saying he'd never get his place electrified.

The Fox just laughed, saying, "What? You think I'm *stupid*?" He then went on about how he'd fought long and hard to have the electrical cables buried underground, but to no avail.

You win some, you lose some, Foxy shrugged. He showed me a photograph of the beach in earlier days-- before they'd scraped so much sand off to make concrete. He'd fought them on that one, too. (Now they get their sand from Manchineel Bay.)

This is what the Jost Van Dyke Preservation Society is all about, according to Foxy. It seeks to preserve what is unique about Jost-- particularly its rugged natural beauty. Society members believe that much of the attraction of Jost is its 'untouched by modern technology' appearance.

The idea, Foxy says, is to "buy land so everybody can enjoy it. Buy land, and turn it back into park land."

We talked about that, along with other things, as he took me down the road for a tour of his house.

"Sure you don't need shoes?" he asked.

"Nah," I said.

Foxy has that rolling gait that is partial to people who go barefoot often. I'm the other way-- but me feets is hard 'nough.

I asked him about housing on the north side of the island. He said there wasn't any.

Why?

"We haven't been developed like St. Thomas," he said.

That's also part of the Preservation Society. The feeling of many JVDPS members is that the future development of Jost should be channeled in ways which preserve the island's natural flavor while still providing a good quality life for both resident and visitor alike. Foxy also would like to encourage the maintenance of old hiking trails and the creation of new ones. He favors low-impact campgrounds over high-impact condos.

At the moment, almost all the old donkey tracks are overgrown on Jost. They were once vital links between the east and west ends of the island. Foxy remembers a time when, just out of school, he had to work two days a week 'for the Crown' during which he was part of a road clearing crew which maintained the trails. This, of course, was before the road along the south coast came into being.

Foxy thinks that the Preservation Society might act as an

impetus to create some long-term employment for the people of Jost, and allow those citizens to work maintaining the natural beauty of their island-- not destroying it along with their own culture.

I asked him about the Society's start.

He'd been talking about it in the bar, and: "Somebody said, 'Take your hat off, Foxy!' So I did, and it gets passed around and the next thing you know-- there's fifty dollars in it!"

So he next throws a Valentine's Day party, and before you know it they've collected $5,000.

Soon the word was humming along the inter-island coconut telegraph that Foxy was up to something.

The ensuing publicity-- and publicity is something which Foxy has never exactly shied away from-- swept into Jost like an August hurricane. Scotland Yard showed up, along with the chief of detectives from Tortola.

"So, er, Mr. Foxy, we hear you been... er.... *soliciting* funds?"

"Yassir."

"Ah, would you be so kind as to *show* us, eggs-actly, *where* and for *what* these funds are being collected for?"

"Yassir. Right here, boss..."

Foxy and Tessa quickly whipped out the JVD Preservation Society bank book-- clearly showing all the deposits for the new group. It was around this time that Foxy and Tessa realized just how far their original idea had come since its low-key conception. It dawned on them that maybe-- just maybe-- they were on to something big which could have a real impact on preserving the quality of life on Jost.

The end result of this meeting was a realization that they had to get *officially* organized. According to their government visitors, this meant becoming what's known in the BVIs as an NGO, or Non-governmental Organization. This is the same thing as a non-profit organization in the US. It permits an organization like the Jost Van Dyke Preservation Society to legally solicit funds from the public.

Of course, Foxy and Tessa have had some help getting the 'Society' off the ground. Janice Ferry, of the Nature Conservancy, came down last August and spent a month with them. She helped with the original ground work for setting up the organization's structure. She went back to North Carolina to get married, and, Foxy hopes, her family will grow along with JVDPS.

They also went down to Trinidad to attend a workshop on the ecology of small islands, and how fragile they are. There are numerous long-term projects which the 'Society' is just beginning to explore. The fact that some of these projects might take years to accomplish doesn't mean they shouldn't be started soon.

Of course, sometimes the task at hand seems daunting. It would be easy to get discouraged. But Foxy, Tessa, and other concerned members of the JVDPS are up for it. This is their home, and the home of their children. They're interested in its long term future.

Their main support has primarily come from individual people. Win Rockerfeller, Edith Bourne, and James Michener have all pledged their support, along with many others who want to see a special place like Jost survive.

"The main thing is that we've begun," says Tessa. "Some of the organizational work is already under our belt. We're off to a good start. It's really happening. We're actually *doing* something rather than just sitting around and talking about it..."

Indeed they are. At the time of this writing, there is over

$7,000 in the JVDPS kitty. Just a brief time ago, it was only $50 and a vague idea.

But that's Foxy.

When he wants something to happen-- he dusts off his hands, rolls up his sleeve, and *makes* it happen.

One day, as we were walking up the path to Foxy's house, he stopped suddenly.

"See that mango tree?" he says, pointing to a tree a few feet off the path. "That's a 'nigger grave.' You see the bottle hanging up? That's how Europeans kept the slaves out of the trees."

What?

"They would take some dirt from a grave, put it in a bottle and, then hang it in the tree. They'd then tell their slaves that if they went up the tree after the fruit, the slave would soon swell up and die..."

"So the bottle's still there!" I said.

"Yeah," Foxy said with a laugh. "I put it there!"

Foxy recently moved back into the (extensively expanded and remodeled) house he was born in.

He described to me how they'd chopped off the 'legs' of the house, and carefully moved the whole thing until it was alongside the cistern.

Then he started adding various rooms to it, going all the way around the original house. Justine's room is just off the side of the front porch. Christian and Jemilla share a room. There's a bath, shower, and a large airy kitchen-- all of which are clustered around the original one-room structure.

It's a typical Foxy project-- preserving the best from the past while incorporating many of the conveniences of the present.

The entire house is all newly painted with the brightest, cheeriest of colors-- pinks, corals, blues-- traditional West Indian colors.

We stood in the center room which was the original house. "That's where I was born, right in the corner," Foxy said.

I asked him how old he was.

"Well, I came to Jost Van Dyke 54 years ago. That makes me, lets see, 47 years old.... yeah, that's right... last year I was 48 years old... and the year before that, 49..."

Out back behind the house is what Tessa calls the 'Great Wall of China.' Foxy is having a V-shaped wall built, facing uphill, which will cause the water coming down the hill to divert around the house.

Oraldo is building it with some help. He lives on Little Jost with his wife Beverly, her daughter, and her grandchild. Beverly runs the kitchen at Foxy's.

A pickup truck comes rumbling into the yard. It is filled with stones for the wall, and Tessa can sense that they're overanxious to dump it.

"Watch out for the *bougainvillea*!" Tessa cries out, jumping up and running to the edge of the porch.

There's a faint cry of, "Don't worry!"

Later, she discovers they managed to miss *most* of them.

Despite all the work and hassle, Foxy feels the wall will be worth it if it diverts the water away from his house and garden. Foxy has a wonderful garden ringing the house. He's got an amazing number of plant varieties growing there-- everything from pigeon peas to pumpkins. He's even got a lime grafted onto an orange tree-- or is it an orange grafted onto a lime tree?

His plants are all doing well. They obviously bring Foxy-the-Farmer great joy. His garden seems to represent security to him. He feels his plants are growing for the future, that there will always be food for his family if his garden grows.

Foxy also owns, as mentioned, some of the last cattle in Great Harbour-- a bull, cow, and calf. He also has two bulls in East End. Someone else on Jost has a couple of cows too. But the cattle days on Jost are over. Foxy told me the story.

The majority of the cattle on Jost used to go to market on St. Thomas. But in the 1950s, some big supermarket chains opened up stores on St. Thomas. All of a sudden the cattle on Jost conveniently developed this 'fever' and couldn't be imported into the United States any more...

Tessa and I talked about the vagaries of the restaurant and bar business. "We have no idea how many customers we'll see from one day to the next. Sometimes only four people come ashore out of twenty boats in the harbor. And there's six bars on the beach!"

She likes the idea of 'semi-catered affairs which is where a tour packager will send a charter group of four or more boats over to Jost for the night. The packager will know that Foxy will be in attendance, assuring an evening or an afternoon of fun for their people.

"If you know they're coming, you have a chance," Tessa said. "Everything is limited here. Your neighbors are limited, your choices are limited. And if you don't get along with every one on the island... arghhh!"

We talked about attempting to "make it" on a small island that depended on what Foxy calls the '...Yankee dollah'. "It's not easy," said Tessa. "Some people expect everything in 'paradise' to be paradisiacal. It often isn't."

"You know, it's like Murphy's Law," Tessa went on, "when your groceries are sitting on the dock in the hot sun after being offloaded from the ferry-- and you know all the frozen stuff inside is melting-- but you can't get over there to retrieve them because you're tending bar or something..."

Foxy shows up with a couple of photo albums. He's got a faded photograph of his first bar-- a small place located between what is now the Paradise Club and the old Methodist Church. This was the first tourist bar on Jost. The building itself was raised off the ground a couple of feet. It had a galvanized roof and plywood walls. Foxy didn't like that, didn't think the building had quite the right feel. Another factor: it was too close to the church, and the parishioners were starting to complain about the noise.

Foxy wanted a real *beach* bar, an open air place with a thatched roof and wattle walls and a sandy floor. He wanted a place more in tune with its natural environment.

So Foxy built a new bar at his current location on his father's property. That was back in 1968. He called it the Tamarind Bar.

"Some people *still* haven't got the name right," Tessa said. "In certain publications, they still refer to it as Foxy's Den of Iniquity. I think they got that from a T-shirt someone had printed up for a Wooden Boat Regatta."

The old photograph of the 'new' bar shows that the original place wasn't much different from today's. Though various additions have been added over the years, Foxy's Den of (oops!)... Tamarind Bar still maintains its original 'beach bar' charm.

It's a laid-back, casual sort of place which personifies the Caribbean for a lot of visitors. When people stroll in for the first time, it is almost as if they've strolled onto a movie set. Some of them can't seem to believe that places like this actually exist anymore.

There is a lot of stuff to look at. T-shirts and clothing are jumbled together with old boat parts. The walls are filled with faded photographs. Many of the autographed and inscribed photographs are of Foxy and/or people who have become his friends. There are people like James Michener, Burt Lancaster,

John Travolta-- and plenty of pretty girls, of course. And there are also some great shots of famous sailing vessels. Everywhere you look there are postcards, paintings, and the ubiquitous business cards people leave behind like personalized litter.

This stuff, all this Foxy memorabilia, has gradually been woven into the warp and woof of the bar. Of course, sometimes things 'disappear'. With so much daily foot traffic, this is bound to happen. Still, it hurts.

Foxy wanted to show me a group photograph of the first Wooden Boat Regatta-- but it was MIA when he went in search of it. It had been on the ceiling near the bar, but the spot where it had been was now empty.

He was clearly angered by the discovery of the theft. The photo had been inscribed to him personally, and was part of both the regatta and the bar's history.

"This is terrible," Foxy said. "May he have trouble, whoever he is! May he have bad luck and don't know where it's coming from! May he always want a *dollah*!"

There's a lot of old photos of Foxy and Tessa around the bar, snapshots of their children, weddings, friends and funerals. There's a lot of nostalgia here-- particularly for a certain style of Caribbean life which is so rapidly changing.

There's even a photo of the start of the first Wooden Boat Race. Bill Coffman (of Rob Roy) had shown up that afternoon we had the one album out, and he, Tessa, and Foxy played the laid-back game of name-that-boat...

We were talking about the 1970's now, and they had some photos of F-4's flying quite closely overhead.

"Oh, yes," Tessa said. "They flew out of Rosy Roads in Puerto Rico. They used to buzz us all the time. The pilots would eventually cruise in by boat-- for a lot of them were sailors-- just dying to meet the man whose new roof they were using as an imaginary bombing target."

Foxy said at times they'd fly so low they'd make rooster tails in the harbor-- sucking the water right up behind them. He remembered one time in particular, when Baba, of Ali Baba's, went backwards right off the dock watching one of the jets streaking over the harbor.

And so another generation of sailors met Foxy, and fell in love with Jost Van Dyke.

Seven generations of Callwoods have called Jost home. There are only eleven main family names here-- we tried getting them all down one afternoon. It wasn't easy. There's the Callwoods, of course, a major contingent. Chinnery is another name I heard a lot. Then Hendricks, George, Maddox, Graham, Coakley, Martin, Milliner, Brewster, and Sewer.

Looking over the photographs in the Callwood family album I was struck by the number of smiling folks who seemed utterly contented. There was one particularly striking black and white of Foxy as a young man. "Yes," Tessa said. "Sidney Hunt took that picture of Fox when he was young and handsome."

What happened?

"I got married," Foxy says. "*Got mah-reeed!*"

We all laughed at that. There was a wonderful feeling of nostalgia as we thumbed through those old albums.

"That was really a wild bunch of people back then," Tessa said. "All the rummy crowd from Tortola, the lushes, the half-crazy ones-- they used to all come over here to party." She said this, though, with a wistfulness, and a fond longing for those begone days.

I mentioned Dave Braisted, who I had met by accident in St. Thomas. Tessa told me about the place he and his wife Shirley had over on the bay across from Little Jost Van Dyke years ago.

She and Foxy went there one time, and watched a pair of 'fishermen'...

"They were running up and down in the water with these cutlasses. I thought they were crazy! They're gonna catch a fish?"

"Yeah," Foxy added. "Running up and down, cryin' out, running through the water!"

It so happens that they *were* fishing-- chasing trunk and bone fish. One acted as a foil, driving the fish towards his partner. The cutlass was their preferred method of capture in the shallows-- swift, and to the, er, point.

"In those days," Tessa recalls, "You always had someone to talk about... every day there was a major story about what happened the night before. All those charter skippers used to hang out in Yacht Haven at Fearless Fred's when they weren't here. They all knew each other..."

The standard small crewed charter operation in those days usually consisted of a couple-- many of them married and with children-- sailing their own boat.

"And some of them were *both* crazy," Tessa remembers. "There was no telling who was going to end up with who the next morning..."

Foxy said something about the charter business being a chosen lifestyle. He went on to discourse on the reality of the average person's work-a-day world-- where they have to work all year to get a two week vacation.

"*Give me a break*, you know what I mean?" he lamented. He wasn't knocking hard work, but he couldn't understand how someone could *allow* themselves to fall into such a rut.

"I'm sorry," Foxy says. "If that's the way of the world, I refuse to join!"

The Wooden Boat Race

Memory confounds the demands of narrative,
certainty is a casualty of memory...
John Gregory Dunne

Ah, wood boats! Back in the days when men were men and boats where hewn out of deciduous and coniferous plant life-- things were different!

Indeed.

Today, most pleasure boats in the Caribbean are not lovingly crafted out of wood. Instead they are poured out of a barrel like so much...

What did L. Francis Herrshoff call it?

Yes-- *frozen snot*!

"All the sailors who drank here were always complaining that there was no chance for a wooden boat to *win* any of the local races anymore," Tessa reminisced.

We were lounging about her porch one sunny afternoon, going through the 'files'-- old photographs, articles, letters, lists, and race cards of past regattas. All the musty and salt-laden 'stuff' documenting the 20 year history of one of the Caribbean's most famous sailing events.

Yes, you got it, folks... *Foxy's Wooden Boat Regatta*!

I began learning about the Regatta by spending the morning

in the bar going over the perpetual trophies. I studied the names and dates on their little brass plates. I marvelled at the ingenuity of many of the more unusual trophies-- no gold, silver, or pewter bowls and goblets here, no ersatz *cups*.

Collectively, they tell a story. Many of them harken back to the bygone days of working sail. There's an old wooden block, a long oar, a small rudder, a bronze porthole, a piece of rigging, a *hand* carved out of wood, a simple plywood board, a rough hewn piece of *lignum vitae* with a belaying pin...

Oops. There *is* a cup, after all. They *do* have a place in yachting tradition. It's fashioned out of wood, of course.

But let's *go* back a bit. Just *how* did all this craziness start? Why does the population of this tiny island literally explode every Labor Day... when it's not even a holiday weekend in the British Virgin Islands....

"Well," Tessa said, "Bill Bodle was of the idea that it should be like.... everybody has a few drinks, swims out to their boats, and just starts sailing. That was *really* the essence of the start of the regatta."

There were seven boats in the first Wooden Boat Race-- depending on who is counting. There was Greg Birra on *Tiki*, of "Adventures in Paradise" fame ("Leaky Tiki, we used to call her," Foxy says). Joe Garrison on *Taormina*.

Bill Bodle, of course, had the *Grace* then. His old schooner, the *Nordlyes*, was the schooner Foxy sailed off into the sunset (sunrise?) aboard to find a wife.

Peter Watson, with Les Anderson on board, sailing *Spartan*.

And *Thetis*, a fiberglass (?) sloop owned by Guy and Dotty Vaughn from St. John. In the true spirit that Foxy's Wooden Boat Regatta has come to personify, *Thetis* was invited to race along despite her being 'plastic', the field being that small.

The famous St. Johnian Block Island Cowhorns came along

the next year, with Les Anderson sailing his own *Penelope* and Augie Holland in *Taurus*. But maybe that second year was really the first year? About the only thing that is absolutely certain about the Regatta, is that not many of the people who were actually there are still certain about *anything*!

Bill Coffman remembers *Shellback* and *Windigo* being in evidence also, but admits to not racing himself until 1976.

The truth often gets a tad elusive on Jost. We were pouring over the Callwood's photo albums, looking for clues. Bill said, "See, that's *Windigo*, there," pointing to a sail in a small fuzzy black and white photograph.

"No, that's *Spartan*," Foxy said.

And Tessa then asked Bill, "Everybody on *Rob Roy* takes pictures-- do you have any?"

Bill just gave her a blank look. Then he said, "Not really. You know, it's funny having a big old wooden boat. People come on board, step over, around, and on you-- until finally asking me, 'Who the hell *are* you, anyway?'"

As usual, Tessa is a fountain of interesting information. She digs out an old article she wrote for Caribbean Boating about the Regatta's tenth anniversary. From selected sections of her original manuscript...

When the race was that small the competing skippers simply chose one of their number to conduct the skipper's meeting. They agreed on the course (simple) and the rules (few). This simplicity proved quite satisfactory, and is probably why the race today is still conducted over the same course.

Chairman of the first two skipper's meetings was Captain Bill Bodle. He was a charterboat owner, skipper, schooner lover, and genuine adventurer. At that time he owned the schooner

Grace and currently (we think) has the *Panda*. A longtime friend of Foxy's from his earliest bar days, it was Bill Bodle who had persuaded Foxy to temporarily abandon his bar and help him sail the schooner *Nordlys* (designed by Ford, Payne, and Roue) to the Mediterranean for the summer charter season...

After the first two years, Bodle's overseas charter schedule prevented him from being in the area on the new dates set for the race-- Labor Day weekend in September. (The first two Regattas were held in March) Interest in the race was already growing-- and having to handle the race, party, publicity, sponsors, donors of prizes and trophies was more than Foxy had bargained for.

The 1976 Regatta bore out the "looseness" of the proceedings (and) almost led to a "falling apart"-- with less than favorable reports.

"The skipper's meeting was an incidental gathering" (see VI Boating, No 12, 1976). Sailors were grumbling over the general disorganization and people were getting the idea that it was just a "come and do as you please party."

This prompted Foxy in 1977 to ask some long-time boating friends from Tortola-- Albie Stewart, Bill Hirst, George Forster, and Robin Tattersall-- to help him organize the race in a more formal manner. Foxy felt by involving local racing enthusiasts the race would be assured of becoming a permanent event on Jost Van Dyke.

The basic idea was to stage an event during which all the lovers of wooden boats-- both traditional and modern-- could come together to race on Jost.

"After all," said Foxy, "Jost Van Dyke is a part of the BVI and we have to accede to the laws there, so we needed a group of respected citizens (no Brethren of the Coast, these) to represent us to the government and to provide an orderly and organized approach, so that certain elements who considered

89

the purpose of the Regatta to be 'just have a good time and doing whatever you want' (see VI Boating, No 12, 1976) would not have the effect of ruining the event for genuine wooden boat lovers and race enthusiasts."

There was even some vague talk of moving the Regatta out of the BVIs-- but it came to nothing.

Despite some temporary disillusionment, Foxy endured. But he also decided it was time to separate himself somewhat from the Regatta for a year or two... to allow anyone who felt they had a stronger right than he... to hold it wherever they wanted.

"Consequently," says Foxy, "after two more years of the Regatta being held but with an apparent decline in the original spirit of the event, it would seem that the time has come to form a Permanent Committee to ensure that the original spirit is preserved."

The Tortola group gave freely of their time and energy to help organize the race from 1977 to 1980 when reports were again much more favorable. Entries were down after continued postponements due to Hurricanes David and Frederick in 1979. This made Foxy less than keen to continue holding the event right in the middle hurricane season.

Foxy proposed an Executive Committee to be formed to run the actual race itself. Hopefully, this will include Mike McFarlan and other members of the West End Yacht Club who did such a good job last year-- both by maintaining the traditional course and adding a Single Handed Race which will be included again this year.

Foxy also put forward the motion for consideration of a possible alternative out-of-hurricane-season date for the event-- but everyone (including Foxy) decided it should be the participants themselves who decided the matter!

Despite the fact that it entailed more work for the committee members (who naturally prefer the fun of racing over the work), Robin Tattersall proposed that a simple handicap system be introduced to give traditionally slower boats a better chance. Both he and Bill Hirst will work out the method along with Mike and other members of the Executive Committee.

Plans are also in the making to direct funds which could feasibly be raised at such a time to benefit the local community.

Since Jost is a small island with not even the bare bones of an economy yet in existence, Foxy would like to see local residents benefit not only from the additional dollars the race nets for local businesses, but also by directing any other revenues which might be forthcoming towards worthwhile local projects-- either to help enhance the island's natural beauty, to benefit the local church, or to contribute to some much-needed community facilities.

So Tessa Callwood had her say on the matter of the Regatta. It's all water over the lee rail now, but there *was* quite a bit of controversy at the time. This year's (1992) event, however, with 30+ entries, coinciding with the 10th Annual JVD Festival, was all Foxy and Tessa had envisioned back in the early 1980's when things looked, well, bleak...

As Caribbean Boating's Gary Metz writes about this year's race, "Traditionalists displayed and/or raced their gaff-rigged varnish-laden beauties with well-earned pride; modern-rigged classics managed impressive performances; and the sleek multihulls danced around the courses... on shore, you could arrive by ferry, ignore the racing, and still have a perfectly good time enjoying Jost's 10th annual festival."

There were over two hundred boats in the harbor this year. And next year will be the Regatta's 20th anniversary, coinciding with Foxy's 25th anniversary-- it should be quite a party!

As we sat around, chewing the mainbrace (we being myself, Foxy, Bill Coffman, Paul Morrel, and Tessa)-- Tessa said, "With next year being the 25th anniversary of the bar, you guys should come up with some wild and crazy ways for us to celebrate! You're not skydivers, are you?"

"Hell, I'd love to jump out of an airplane," Bill Coffman quipped.

Tessa described the 'jump' they had on the 20th anniversary. "They formed FOXY in the sky as they jumped, and landed perfectly!"

And there were other suggestions, such as having a race where the boats had to sail over the starting line backwards. "We're good at that," Bill said.

But on a more serious side, Tessa mentioned that there had been a suggestion for a board sailing event. "Do you think that would be appropriate?"

The consensus was that it would be-- particularly if it was staged as a spectator event. A course could be set up right in the harbor. Foxy added that he thought it wouldn't detract from the regular sailing event.

"We want more events," Tessa stated. And when someone suggested how 'the beach games were great this year!', Tessa agreed, saying, "Well, *somebody organized it*, and it went off well."

Bill Coffman said he had to be going. "I've got to hit it-- I want to get back in time for lunch with my wife."

It was nearing noon, and I wondered just how he'd be getting back to Tortola so quickly.

"Well," he said, "It took us exactly nine minutes to get over here-- I had to slow down 'cause of the chop."

Say what?

Bill smiled, then told us about his new craft, "We came over on a little power boat I built. It is cold-molded-- a modified deep vee with a hundred horse on it. Weighs 700 pounds. In a flat calm we were hitting about 45 knots."

"Are you getting into powerboat racing?" Tessa asked.

Bill just smiled again. He owns the Woodworks in West End, on Tortola, and is also well known as the owner and skipper of the famous *Rob Roy*. The big yawl, all fifty-six foot of her, is kept in Bristol fashion, as one might expect with Bill's facilities at the Woodworks. Fine wood boats are his forte-- regardless of how they are powered.

Some of us remember *Rob Roy* from the days she raced on Long Island Sound. Another old friend of mine, Paul Tooker, crewed on her back in the sixties when she garnered her share of prizes. Bill Coffman is keeping alive her fine reputation as a fast racer. During the last Regatta he won the Single Handed event, along with a first in the 50' to 60' modern rig class.

She's a big and fast classic yacht, and a sight to see as she charges along.

During the last Regatta I was fortunate to sail aboard Julien Davies' *Tiger Maru*, a cold molded 37' sloop. We were the first monohull to cross the line, and just ahead of *Rob Roy*. She looked magnificent as she charged along behind us with a bone in her teeth...

Just as Bill and Paul were leaving, Tessa asked, "Are you guys going to be members of the JVD Preservation Society?"

"Sure. Soon as I get a hundred bucks," said Bill.

"Membership won't be that high. We want as many members as we can get..."

It's interesting to think about the parallels between the

Wooden Boat Regatta and JVD Preservation Society. Both are devoted to preserving wonderful things which were about to disappear forever. The Regatta honors the old wooden boats and the salt-stained people who sail them. The JVD Preservation Society seeks to protect the natural beauty of a special island, and honor the rich cultural traditions of its unique people. It is no coincidence that the driving force behind both of these far-sighted visions are the same two people, Tessa and Foxy Callwood.

Many years ago, a young man sailed into Jost. He arrived at dusk. There was little wind. It was a beautiful evening. The harbor was very quiet. The stars were bright. The island looked so peaceful and serene in the gathering darkness....

On shore, he could hear hymns coming from the church. A couple of natives on the end of the dock were singing some type of calypso, accompanying themselves on guitars.

'What could be more perfect than this.' thought the young man at the helm of his 28' wooden cutter. The island before him was almost heart-breakingly beautiful. It seemed unreal. It was the very epitome of the Caribbean he had sailed so many miles to find.

Suddenly, the two natives on the end of the dock began singing loudly, "Go back, mon! Go back! De water she getting *tin*!"

'How quaint', thought Neil Lewis. His boat was dead in the water-- completely still. There wasn't a breath of air. He went forward...

"I started to put the anchor into the water," Neil recalled many years later, "but it wouldn't *go* in the water. I realized I was aground, and the water was, indeed, too *thin*!"

Lewis had gently slid up on the old sandy reef off the beach at Great Harbour. No damage was done, except perhaps to his pride.

"That was the first time I became aware of his existence," Neil said, speaking of Foxy Callwood. For it had been Foxy and Ruben singing on the end of the dock. (Yes, the same Ruben who has gone on to musical fame.)

The year was 1962.

Today, Neil Lewis is the captain and owner of the *Alexander Hamilton*. She is a traditional native schooner which Neil had built exclusively for the day charter trade. She's beautifully laid out, open on deck, and US Coast Guard certified to carry 38 passengers. He likes to keep his charter operation first class.

"We're on the upper end," he says. He and his crew, Katherine, start off serving their passengers fresh coffee (none of that *instant* stuff), orange juice, and Danish at 9 a.m.

Later in the morning there are plantains, pickles, and a selection of pastries served. Dinner is fresh roast beef ("I cook over a *ton* of roast beef a year!"), roast chicken, pasta salad, and even puffed pastries with raspberry filling.

"Everything is carved at the table," Lewis says. The table is covered with linen cloth and adorned with glass and silver cutlery-- all rather unusual on a day-charter boat.

Their guests have a choice of imported champagnes and wines, along with other beverages. Afterwards, there's freshly-brewed coffee again, with a variety of liqueurs.

"We spoil 'em!"

Neil says he grew up in the food business. He spends over an hour a day just cooking-- he steams the shrimp, roasts the beef and poultry, bakes the pastries- and this is just the *food* preparation for a day's sail.

"If we can't do it top quality-- we don't do it!"

But that's the type of unique charter character Neil Lewis is. While the 'bean-counters' on the other day-charter boats spend their time seeking ways of giving their customers *less*, Neil spends *his* time laboring in the kitchen so they will have *more*!

Perhaps that's one of the secrets to his long-term success. He's been in the charter business in the VI longer than anyone else.

Born in Saratoga Springs ("Right near the race track!"), Neil certainly qualifies as an expert on the chartering scene in the VI. "It's not an easy profession," he admits. "especially if you intend to really make a living at it. I've managed to *live*, but haven't made a *living*!"

The building of the *Alexander Hamilton* is itself a wonderful story. Lewis is currently writing a book about it, and sections of his manuscript have already been excerpted in local publications. However, the writing is going slower than expected. "Now that I've got the *boat*, I've no time to write the *book*!"

Neil is a traditionalist. His boat reflects that attitude. The *Alexander Hamilton* was built on the beach in Nevis using traditional island shipbuilding methods-- adze, ax, plane, and handsaw-- by local island shipwrights.

Even its name has a story. Both the man (Alexander Hamilton) and the boat were born on the island of Nevis. Both then moved to the Virgin Islands. The man Alexander Hamilton went to St. Croix, while the boat went to its home base in Red Hook on St. Thomas.

As Neil puts it, however, there the similarities stop. For Hamilton then "...moved to New York, got to be a big wheel in government, went over to New Jersey, and got blown away!"

Alexander Hamilton, besides being somewhat of an elitist (*Hamiltonianism* holds as one of its political principles a general distrust of the political capacity or wisdom of the common man), is, of course, known for losing a duel to another lawyer, Aaron Burr. This duel wasn't held in a courtroom, however, but along the Hudson Palisades just after dawn in 1803.

So much for early American history.

Speaking of history, I asked Neil his version of the beginnings of the Wooden Boat Race and Foxy's in general. He thinks there may have been some type of grudge match involved, but the whole thing has gotten so hazy over the years it hardly seems to matter.

Neil and Foxy became friends soon after the first bar-- the one near the Methodist church-- opened in Great Harbour. As Neil remembers it, "The hymn singing on Sunday morning disturbed the bar people who had hangovers!"

So back in '68, Foxy moved 'lock, stock, and barrel' down the beach to where his current Tamarind Beach Bar and Restaurant now stands.

So what were the old days like? What was Foxy like in those days? Who was he?

"We had *some* times," Neil said. "Foxy was a bit of a hellraiser. We had a lot of fun.

"When he first started to do the big parties, I *loved* his style! He would run around for a week beforehand, totally organizing and delegating everything-- so everybody *knew* exactly what to do. By the time the party started, he'd just get roaring drunk until he couldn't stand up anymore... or maybe even disappear-- letting off all the stress and worry of the previous week. He's changed *that* style a lot, though."

Because of Foxy, Great Harbour was becoming known among the charter crowd as a good overnight anchorage. Things were usually jumping at the Tamarind, and, if they weren't-- all you had to do was rustle up Foxy Callwood and the party was on!

Neil remembers quite a few nights with the Fox sharing one end of his boat-- and never without feminine companionship. "I remember when he married Tessa," Neil said, shaking his head. Then, laughing, "And gave up one part of his *wicked, wicked* ways!"

The first Wooden Boat Race which Neil participated in occurred while he was building his house in Red Hook. He was sailing the *Red Hooker* then, a 28' island sloop with a 12' beam. "Like a pumpkin seed," he says.

The *Hooker* had been built on Beef Island for Caneel Bay to carry cargo. All the fruit trees planted on Sandy Cay were brought there aboard her. But Neil didn't buy the boat from Caneel...

"Sonny Diamond had it awhile," Neil told me. "He had a couple of local bars-- Upchucks and Morningstar Beach. Married some girl, then ran off with her mother..."

I smiled at this.

"Yeah, lots of good stuff!" Neil said laughing. He was still dressed in his sailing uniform-- a bathing suit and a starched white shirt tied at his hard belly. The interior of the *Alexander Hamilton* is comfortable. It's a clean and nicely laid out saloon.

"Anyway," Neil went on, "Sonny was tall, square-jawed, and told me once that he'd been a gigolo since the age of fourteen."

"I met him at a party in 1954, in Richmond, Virginia. He rode into the party on his motorcycle. Trouble was, the party was in a brownstone on the third floor! He was there with Charlie Brown-- who had Fat City-- and they came roaring in. They had an awful time getting that motorcycle back down...

"Actually, I bought the boat through Charlie Brown. Sonny had already been arrested or something on the Canadian border, but that's another story..."

So Neil's first Wooden Boat Race was on the *Red Hooker*.

The "*Hooker*" came after his first charter boat, *Arawak*. That was another native sloop, some 29 feet in length. His first-girl, first-mate at the time was Les Anderson's girlfriend's sister.

At the time, Les was still sailing his first boat *Banshee*. "Yes, I've done a lot of sailing, a lot of partying on *Banshee*," Neil remembers.

But, back to the race. "We took the propeller off, figuring we'd need all the speed we could get. I waited on the dock here in Red Hook for my wife, and we were supposed to leave just after noon. But we had a lot of beer on board, and by the time she arrived at 6:30, we were pretty loaded."

"So we sailed out of Red Hook, and arrived at Jost in the dark. We were feeling pretty good. We tacked all the way up to the beach. We were determined to get as close to the dock as possible. We got about twenty feet closer to shore than Les. He didn't like that!"

Neil smiled throughout the story. He and Les Anderson have had an easy-going rivalry for some twenty years now.

Neil didn't do too badly in the race, considering. His boat was a Marconi-rigged native sloop so it was classified as non-traditional. Only gaff-rigged vessels were classified as 'traditional'.

Since they had missed the skipper's meeting, Neil didn't know the course. So they followed a little native sloop called *Driftwood*, which was owned by the Johnson brothers of Coral Bay, St. John. And, if they had only known the course, they could have laid a mark much earlier and *probably* would have won in the traditional class..

"But, whatever," Neil says now. "We had fun!"

While sailing back home the next day, the wind died. His sweet little engine wasn't much good without a propeller!

But Neil had learned something interesting during the race. He'd experimented with running his mainsail loose-footed on the boom, and discovered that he gained a whole knot. So Neil kept the mainsail loose-footed.

Unfortunately, this must have added a slightly different strain on the spar because a couple of weeks later the boom developed a large crack and almost snapped in two.

He was on charter at the time, so he sent his charter party ashore to snorkel, and then commenced gluing and screwing the boom back together. He then motored home, and sailed it the next day.

"That was the only repairs it ever got! That was the way it was *done* in those days...."

In 1984, the *Alexander Hamilton* was finished. Though Neil didn't 'officially' enter the Wooden Boat Race that year, he sailed along with it. Some of the big old Baltic Traders were there, like the *Elinor*.

"We sailed circles around them! They didn't know who we were. We weren't on the race sheet or anything."

That sounded impressive to me. The *Alexander Hamilton* is a 28 ton vessel drawing only five feet of water. However, as Neil says, "It's amazing how well she'll do if she has some breeze and no seas!"

We also talked about writing, and getting people to tell their stories.

"What I'd like to do (and have talked and talked about) is to get these guys up to my house for a party.... I talking about the guys who were here when I came back in '62... get them drinking and telling stories... and then tape record the whole thing."

I thought that was a great idea....

"But then," Neil said with a laugh, "most of them can't stand each other. Never could!"

"The real old-timers aren't me and Les and Foxy. We're the new-timers. The old-timers are Dave Braisted, Don Street, Augie Holland, Basil Simonette-- those guys."

Neil told me that Basil Simonette claims to have taken the

first VI charter party out in 1945 or '46. "He's the son of Sir Roland Simonette who used to own the whole Bahamas...."

A few days after my conversation with Neil, I went hiking on the east end of St. John and visited Les Anderson.

Les is currently building a house just to the east of Moor Point. The main structure is set just below the ridge line. It has a southern exposure. Hurricane Hugo blew away much of his previous structure, and Les is making sure this house is built to last.

Les is a painter. His work is well-known throughout the Caribbean for its distinct island flavor.

I carefully picked my way down the path to the house. There are stone steps built into the hillside, and along the path are pieces of glass, coral, rock, artifacts, old tools, and odd bits of equipment that have caught Les's fancy during the twenty-two odd years he's been living in the Caribbean.

Today, Les is working on the bathroom plumbing. His lot is a steep one. Each time Les drops a tool, it skitters fifty feet down the slope before being caught by the vegetation. You can hear the surf breaking just a couple of hundred feet below. It is a dramatic setting for a home.

Les is 48 years old now, yet still retains a certain boyishness charm. He has a slightly bashful manner, as if he's about to tell a particularly outrageous story. You can sense from his easy-going, laid-back attitude that he has no secrets he won't reveal-- *if* he can remember them.

"Have a seat," he says as he catches sight of me. "Put your bag down... would you like a soda?"

I start off by asking him about *Banshee*, the first boat he owned here in the VI.

"Well, that's a 'gray' area!" Les replied, laughing.

He did tell me she was a Cape 25 which had been built in Durban some 70 years ago. She was a pilot cutter, and built to withstand the strong South African winds which blew around the Cape of Good Hope.

Les used to sail her over to Foxy's just about every week. He was building his schooner *Penelope* at the time. (*Penelope* is his Block Island Cow Horn which is often moored in Round Bay.)

He recalls the first race at Foxy's as essentially a contest between *Spartan* and *Taormina*. "It was just a boat race - no one declared it a wooden boat race at first," Les said. "Then Foxy-- you know how Foxy is-- decided to make it an *event*!"

Les agrees the first race was bereft of the Coral Bay Cowhorns.

Les went on, "Augie challenged me the following year. He wanted a boat to race. It was the first time we locked horns, as it were. The name of his boat was 'Taurus!'"

Augie is August Holland, one of the progenitors of the nefarious St. John Cowhorns. Currently, his new boat, another Cowhorn, sports a fully-battened rig.

Les designed the T-shirts for the first event-- a tradition he continues today. Back then he was not only designing them, but manually printed them as well. "I made a hundred wood-block hand printed shirts," he says. "That was the first organized race."

"So, how'd you do against Augie?"

Les took a breath in, then let it out saying, "I won 'em!" We laughed. Then he said, "He beat me the next year, though..."

"The whole thing was started by a couple of guys sitting around Foxy's drinking and talking and complaining," said Les, "Those of us who owned wooden boats were always complaining that there wasn't a race in which our boats could be competitive. Sure, the St. Thomas Yacht Club sponsored some races out of Cowpet Bay, but their light fiberglass boats were a lot faster than ours..."

I knew already, of course, but what else?

"Foxy was definitely the instigator. He'd get you all excited, and then just sit back and watch you do it!"

Les sailed on *Spartan* during the first race. She was a New York 50 designed by Nat Herreshoff. "It was *Spartan* against *Taormina*-- I remember that. It was just an impromptu thing. Foxy got the big boats together, and they just went for a little 'beer can' race. I don't remember there being more than five or six boats."

Les remembers other encounters. "One time, we raced *Spartan* and *Cotton Blossom* to St. Croix for the afternoon! When you're doing 12 knots or so, 40 miles is nothing."

I said something to the effect that St. Croix was a long way.

"That was not an uncommon thing at the time. The boats happened to be there, and we just went for it!"

I asked if he had any T-shirts left from that first race. "God, no. They fell by the wayside. I had the block I used to print them for a few years. That was a big job, hand-blocking a hundred shirts. But I sold them all!"

We talked about his new house. Les is proud of its progress. We sat in the main room, which he thinks will probably serve as his artist studio for a while. The view is incredible. St. Croix was visible to the south, the sun sparkling hotly on the sea like white-hot lava.

I asked what he was working on now, art-wise. "As far as painting, I am not," he said glumly. "It's very frustrating, but right now the house comes first. You gotta have a place to live..."

The interior woodwork of the house is all South American hardwood. The ceiling beams are carved from particularly heavy timbers, and all the wood is naturally finished. The stone work is done in the West Indian style, with pieces of rock and coral and shell worked into the design. Les is obviously into 'making art' no matter what he does.

He described the wood he used while building his schooner *Penelope* as Gommeez, a wood from the island of Dominica. It was similar to the wood he is using for the house, but not as resinous.

"The grain goes like this..." and he waves his hands around in circles. "It's a power-planer job. You try not to use a hand plane on it."

The maiden voyage for *Penelope* was Foxy's Wooden Boat Race. He won. "A lot of hazy days in those days," Les says. "But those were some *great* times!"

I found Bill Hirst in his office at Fort Burt, right next door to the Paradise Pub.

Bill Hirst is an easy man to talk to. I first spoke to him by phone a few days before our meeting, and he beguiled me with interesting stories right away. He's a straight-forward-type-of-guy.

So, I asked him, straightforwardly, what was his first contact with Foxy's Wooden Boat Regatta.

"I had a *Carol* ketch at the time. She was a double-ender--sort of a scaled down Tahiti ketch. They were slow boats... a friend of mine used to say, 'They won't drown you, but they might starve you!'"

"Anyway," Bill said, "I was doing some salvage work on a 37 foot boat from Puerto Rico which had burned right in harbour of Jost. We were given the hull - Foxy, Albert (Stewart), and myself."

He had sailed over on his double-ended ketch, of course. She was a classic wooden boat if there ever was one. "Somebody rowed over and said, 'Hey, we're going to have a race, would you like to join?'-- that type of thing. I declined. I was too busy taking the treasure off this boat we had the rights to..."

Bill raced in later Regattas, both with and without his ketch. Along with Robin Tattersall, Albie Stewart, and George Forster-- Bill Hirst was part of that early race committee which helped keep the fledgling Wooden Boat Race afloat in those first wild and crazy years of the Regatta.

Foxy knew that he had a tiger by the tail after the first few years of the Regatta. And, he knew that in order to keep this tiger from eating him, he had to get well organized, race-wise. For this, he relied on those he knew best along the Tortola waterfront.

"We ran the first few races," said Bill. "Robin Tattersall was always racing-- always had a wooden boat. It was fun."

Bill donated a perpetual trophy for Foxy's, and its story is typical of the relationship between these friends.

"Robin Tattersall had a Herreshoff Bull's Eye at one time. It's now somewhere on the bottom of the sea between Cooper Island and Roadtown. The Bull's Eye is an open boat, you know."

"His children (Tattersall's) had left Cooper Island one day, and they just *sailed it in*! A big squall came up and she went *down*. They swam around for over two hours.

"Now the rudder I gave Foxy for the trophy was a spare rudder for that Herreshoff Bull's Eye. It was built right here in the woodshop. It had been roughly shaped by David Smith for Robin as a replacement rudder.... but, well, then the boat *sank*!

"It was in an unfinished state, so I begged it and I finished it off. I thought it would be a good trophy for the Wooden Boat Race."

Indeed.

We talked a bit about those early days-- the first wild Wooden Boat Regattas. "It was crazy. Labor Day isn't a holiday here in the BVI. All the sailors from St. Thomas were ready to keep on partying, but we BVI sailors had to get back to work!"

Jost was still a one-sheriff island in those days. "Albert Chinnery was the only government agent-- like Cap'n Smith on Anegada. There was only one phone. If you wanted to phone anybody, you had to go through the government agent."

Bill mentioned that Foxy was a 'local constable' for many years. I heard Foxy sing of such, but I never thought of the reality. But the Fox still has his hat, badge, truncheon, and all..!

I had Bill Hirst establish my bonafides with Albie Stewart over the phone from his office. Albie Stewart is a busy man, and runs a tight ship at Tortola Yacht Services.

"I've know Foxy since 1965." said Albie. "We've been friends a long time. The Regatta just grew and grew, and at some point Foxy asked us to help out with the staging of the race..."

"...We've had some fascinating committee boats. We used Elizabeth Taylor's big yacht *Kilizma* for one race. It was loaned to us by the Japanese, who had purchased it from the Burton's."

"The Regatta has totally been an effort by the Callwoods and the people of Jost Van Dyke. Tattersall, Hirst, and I just helped out with the technical end of the racing."

I asked about that, particularly the handicapping system used.

"It was extraordinarily informal at first-- we didn't use any handicap system. Then, after awhile, we *did* attempt to handicap the boats. But there was a great deal of resistance to it. They wanted to go back to the old form of just... pickup and race!"

I knew that Robin Tattersall and Bill Hirst had worked out a handicapping system similar to one used in the St. Barths

Regatta.

"They wanted to keep it very informal, but by then people were really starting to race, to take it seriously."

"We kept the system simple. We had to define modern boats and older boats-- that in itself was hard to determine. But we did it, we sat in those committees and did it..."

On a different note I asked Albie Stewart about the time Foxy thought he needed an operation.

Foxy had already told me the first part, where he made it over to the old Poop Deck in Roadtown to find Dr. Robin Tattersall...

"Doc," Foxy cried to Tattersall, "I need an operation! Gotta take me for an operation..."

Of course, everyone just laughed thinking it was just Foxy kidding around as usual. But Dr. Robin Tattersall could sense Foxy was serious, and told Foxy to meet him at the hospital.

Once there, in the old hospital in Roadtown, Tattersall ran a few tests. Sure enough, Foxy's appendix had to come out!

"But that weekend I had to *pah-tee*!" Foxy recalls. "And so I had to get home! It was a full moon party..."

Albie Stewart filled me in on the rest of it: "Robin operated on him in the old hospital. Foxy couldn't take that hospital. Robin called me about five o'clock in the evening and said, 'I can't keep him here any longer. He's gotta get out!'"

"So I said, 'What'll we do?'"

"'Well,' Dr. Tattersall said, 'we'll lay a board down and strap him to it!'"

Albie Stewart had a 31 foot Bertram at the time named *Big 'Ting*. "We put him in the bottom of the Bertram and took him home!"

Dr. Tattersall and Albie made the run to Jost with Foxy strapped in nice and cozy. "We got him ashore at the bar, and he immediately started to play his guitar!"

And, as Foxy remembers, the good doctor rationed him to

only *three* beers! (Foxy was appreciative!)

"For some reason, " Albie said, "Foxy felt that getting him home saved his life-- that if he had to stay in the hospital another night he couldn't have made it..."

Albie and I then talked about the timing of the race. The middle of the hurricane season seemed like a poor time.

Albie pointed out that the race committee has only postponed the Regatta once due to weather. That didn't seem too bad in twenty years. Foxy's Wooden Boat Regatta has had to endure far more 'heavy weather' from social storms than natural phenomena!

"Labor Day gives them (the racing sailors) their long weekend. All the other weekends are taken up by major events," Albie said, and a quick glace at Caribbean Boating's Sailing Calendar tends to bear this out.

I touched on some of the previous problems that had arisen along with the popularity of the Regatta. Albie mentioned, among other things, that the Festival Village (the annual JVD Festival coinciding with the Wooden Boat Regatta) had helped. "It's spread good will all over Jost."

In that same vein, I asked Albie's opinion of the Jost Van Dyke Preservation Society. He was for it, as long as they "..do it at the level of the people who own the land. It's a big project. The general concept is a good thing for the island. They've opted now *not* to have that pressure to develop commercially. They've opted to really look at the land, the sea, and the access. It's all up to them."

I was interested in how the general BVI business community viewed Foxy and the JVD Preservation Society.

Albert Stewart seemed a good man to ask. He has close ties to the BVI Tourist Board, and his company, Tortola Yacht Services, was awarded the 1991 Business of the Year Award from the BVI Hotel & Commerce Association.

Foxy Callwood was also honored by this same organization

for his "outstanding contribution to entertainment and culture" in the BVI.

"Well," Albie said, in regards to the JVDPS, "generally speaking the Tourist Board seems to be behind it, as well as the Hotel and Commerce Association. I think quite a few people would like to see a good portion of Jost left undeveloped. But its up to the residents of Jost. The people of Anegada feel the same way about their island. We're all-- in one way or the other-- behind people like Tessa and Foxy on issues like this."

But let us not stray too far from the Regatta. From the tattered scraps of rum-stained napkins which Tessa Callwood grandly refers to as her 'Regatta records', comes a list of trophies...

...but, bear in mind, dear reader, that nothing is cast in stone concerning the Wooden Boat Regatta. Even the perpetual trophies seem to come and go, wax and wane, and to occasionally change names, dates, etc.

The following is as 'complete' of a list as possible...

Under 30'	Traditional Class-- Mariner's Inn Tray
	Modern Class-- *Golden Hind* Oar
30-40	Traditional Class-- Tony Edwards Bronze Porthole from the S/V *Robben*
	Modern Class-- Bougainvillea Cup (wood) donated by Dr. Tattersall

40-50	Traditional Class-- Richardson's Marine Rigging block
	Modern Class-- VI Boating (new Caribbean Boating) Plane
50-60	Traditional Class-- Carved Whale by David Walker
	Modern Class-- Norseman Marine Swage (this has since taken over the Bill Hirst rudder trophy, which is retired.)
60+	Traditional Class-- Christian Callwood Trophy (in honor of Foxy's father.)
	Modern Class-- Pusser's Rum Barrel

Multihulls-- Blazing Builders on St. Thomas is donating a trophy for these speedsters, though exactly *what* no one knows as yet!

Island sloops-- Nature's Basket of Jost has donated a traditional woodworker's trim plane.

Foxy's Fastest Monohull-- The lignum vitae belaying pin.

Single-handed race-- A carved wooden hand has been donated by the Woodworks of West End. (They've also donated a trophy for the modern class.)

Confused?

Well, step on board one of these big old wooden babes during a race-- and you'll discover that *confusion* plays a very large part in yacht *racing*....

The actual classes or divisions that the boats race under is decided by their hull and rigs.

The Traditional Class is reserved for those sailing craft sporting gaff rigs. *Gaffers*, they are referred to. You know, they have *lots* of old hemp or galvanized cable for stays and shrouds, and have those funny little booms way up near the masthead.

The Modern Class have fairly 'modern-type' Marconi rigs, whether sloop, schooner, ketch or yawl.

Multi-hulls are just that. They have extra hulls to push through the water, and yet somehow manage to do it rather quickly.

And then there are the island sloops. These are native boats, whether in design or construction, indigenous to the Caribbean and the Bahamas. The *Alexander Hamilton* over in Red Hook is a good example of the type, though it has a schooner rig.

There are not too many of these 'native' craft left. In fact, the total number of wooden boats in existence around the world is rapidly dwindling. Many of the boats which participate in the Wooden Boat Regatta are already relics from the bygone days of 'working sail'.

There are real risks involved in racing such craft.

Awhile back, a renown circumnavigator entered his well-traveled, offshore cruising vessel in the Wooden Boat Regatta. Alas, he cut the vicious north end of Sandy Cay a bit too close, and was soon discovered clinging to his spreaders. The boat, of course, was a total...

...and the locals report that pieces of it are *still* washing ashore on the windward side of Sandy Cay...

All of which just serves to indicate what a crazy event the Wooden Boat Regatta really is-- and just how demented the local VI marine community can be. Many of the vessels participating in the competition should be in museums-- not out at sea bashing through large waves and high winds.

But the Wooden Boat Regatta is also something which is greater than the sum of its parts-- just like Jost itself.

It's more than just a sailboat race-- it's a celebration of a vanishing way of life.

The sailors who founded this regatta were different from the seamen we have floating around the Caribbean today-- they were tougher, more self-reliant, and far more adventurous souls. Their boats were at the very center of their lives. They were equally at home with a sextant, a caulking mallet, and/or a bottle of cheap rum in their hand.

They took large chances, made hard choices, and (occasionally) paid the ultimate price. Most of all, they had *fun*.

And, of course, without realizing it along the way-- they made history. That's what this book is all about.

For the last 25 years, Jost Van Dyke has been their spiritual home-- ever since Foxy Callwood opened up his shabby little beach bar.

Down through the years, all the local charter captains, cruising sailors, and sea gypsies have felt that Foxy's was... well, not just a place in Jost-- but *their* place. They felt they were as much Foxy's guests as his customers. They considered Foxy's an almost magical, unique establishment run by special people on a particularly wonderful island-- where they would always be welcomed with open arms.

For 25 straight years that has been true. And it continues to be true.

Foxy and Tessa have given-- and received-- a lot of love over the course of these many years. And, in return, the island of

Jost Van Dyke has been very good to them, their family, their children, and their many friends. It has nurtured them, fed them, and protected them.

Now, through the coordinated efforts of the Jost Van Dyke Preservation Society, Foxy and Tessa are working to make sure that their *children* and their *children's children* can say the same thing.

They want to leave the island to their children in at least as good physical shape-- if not better-- than when Foxy inherited it from his parents.

They believe that the island of Jost is the collective wealth of its combined inhabitants-- and that it is their duty to invest in its future *now*. They want to work *today* for *tomorrow*. They want the island of Jost Van Dyke to continue to nurture its residents-- not just provide corporate profits for wealthy land speculators.

"It's kindda like a garden," Foxy said once. "With a little bit of care and planning and pruning-- some work and some love-- it will feed you and your family and your friends forever. We're a lucky people here on Jost. It's up to us. We can make things better, or we can stand back and allow them to get worse..."

"...in the end, we'll reap what we sow," he concluded thoughtfully. Then, suddenly, a big smile broke out on his handsome, smiling face. It was as if a bright tropical sun had just peeked through some dark clouds. "Such is Life! Such is Life!" Foxy laughed.

(END)

For more information on the JVDPS, write Foxy at
The Jost Van Dyke Preservation Society
PO Box 37
St. John, VI
00831

American Paradise Publishing is a company devoted to publishing books written *by* Virgin Islanders, *about* Virgin Islanders and *for* Virgin Islanders. Our address: POB 37, St. John, VI 00831 Call (809) 776-8346 or 693-8876 or 776-6922.

ORDER FORM

Chasing the Horizon by Cap'n Fatty Goodlander (4th Printing)
ISBN # 09631060-1-5   Price: $10.00 plus $2.00 S/H

'The Life and Times of a Modern Caribbean Sea Gyspsy'

Seadogs, Clowns, and Gypsies by Cap'n Fatty Goodlander
ISBN # 09631060-2-3   Price: $7.00 plus $2.00 S/H

'Twenty Modern Sea Stories about Colorful Caribbean Characters'

St. John People edited by Cap'n Fatty Goodlander
ISBN # 09631060-5-8   Price: $20.00 plus $2.00 S/H

'A Dozen St. John Writers Profile Twenty Residents'

Sportfishing in the Virgin Islands by Carol Bareuther
ISBN # 09631060-3-1   Price: $10.00 plus $2.00 S/H

'Everything You Need to Know...'

A Taste of the Virgin Islands by Carol Bareuther
ISBN # 09631060-6-6   Price: $16.00 plus $2.00 S/H

'A Cookbook as Diverse, Rich, and Tasty as the Food it Celebrates'

Foxy and Jost by Peter Farrell
ISBN # 09631060-4-X   Price: $12.00 plus $2.00 S/H

'A Man and His Island'